GARDEN ENCHANTMENT

GARDEN ENCHANTMENT
Creative Design With Annuals and Perennials

CHERYL MADDOCKS
Author of *Let the Garden Go*

DOUBLEDAY
Sydney   Auckland   New York   Toronto   London

GARDEN ENCHANTMENT
A DOUBLEDAY BOOK

First published in Australia and New Zealand in 1992 by Doubleday

© Cheryl Maddocks 1992

All rights reserved. No part of this publication may be reproduced, stored in a retrieval system, transmitted in any form or by any means, electronic, mechanical, photocopying, recording or otherwise, without the prior written permission of the publisher.

Maddocks, Cheryl.
Garden enchantment, let the garden go with
annuals and perennials.

ISBN 0 86824 464 3.

1. Annuals (Plants) – Australia. 2. Perennials – Australia.
3. Flowers – Australia. I. Title.

635.930994

Doubleday Books are published by

Transworld Publishers (Aust) Pty Limited
15-25 Helles Avenue, Moorebank, N.S.W. 2170

Transworld Publishers (NZ) Limited
3 William Pickering Drive, Albany, Auckland

Transworld Publishers (UK) Limited
61-63 Uxbridge Road, Ealing, London, W5 5SA

Bantam Doubleday Dell Publishing Group Inc.
666 Fifth Avenue, New York, New York 10103

THIS BOOK WAS PRODUCED BY CHERYL MADDOCKS
EDITED BY JOHN MADDOCKS
Designed by Steven Dunbar
Printed in Hong Kong
through Vantage Graphics, Sydney

Contents

Garden Enchantment 9
Combining for Effect 13
Colour Design 21
The Perennial Border 37
The Versatile Annual 43
The Natural Garden 51
The Magic of Meadows 57
Fragrance in the Garden 61
The Flower Arranger's Garden 67
The Prolific Daisy 71
The Garden at Night 75
The Shade Garden 79
Potted Perfection 87
Herbs in the Garden 91
Edible Flowers 97
Soil Preparation 103
Maintenance 107
Propagation 113
Annuals – a selection list 119
Perennials – a selection list 139
Index 171

I would like to thank the following people for allowing me to photograph their beautfiful gardens. Steven Dean, Steven Melas, Helen Hodgman, Geogina Ligertwood, Heide Park and Art Gallery (Victoria), Everglades (Leura, N.S.W.), Tony and Inga Morphett, Heronswood (Victoria), Colonial Cottage (Kenthurst, N.S.W.), Edoarda Alderighi, June Humphries, Musee de Claude Monet (France), Sissinghurst (England).

Special thanks to John, Celeste and Nicholas

An abundant planting of annuals and perennials

Garden Enchantment

ENCHANTMENT is an elusive quality. Some gardens are well designed and well executed but lack the nebulous qualities that would make them enchanting. The necessary softness, romantic tone and sense of spontaneity are missing.

In many ways, a garden is a retreat from the world, a place in which to find inner repose. I enjoy the satisfaction of knowing that it is my creation, one of the few places in which I am able to bring a distinctive environment into existence. And if a garden is to be a genuine haven, it should have a relaxed and natural feeling. It should be a haven not merely for oneself and one's plants, but for a variety of birds, insects, lizards and butterflies. It should be visually soft, without rigid uniformity or stiffness of plant material. Such a garden will have a slightly unkempt, romantic feeling.

The essential elements of a good garden are design, plant selection and colour combination, but these elements are part of a larger whole. One must complete the garden by adding the necessary depth, by providing the all important detail. The final touch provided by annuals and perennials can be totally responsible for a garden's sense of enchantment.

Trees, shrubs, old-fashioned roses and climbing plants provide structure in the garden. But a garden filled with these components only, no matter how cleverly they are used, may still look flat and uninteresting. A garden in which the spaces between trees and shrubs have been creatively filled with annuals and perennials will contain wonderful combinations and produce remarkable garden pictures. The everchanging, fluid nature of annuals and perennials contributes to a soft, enchanting ambience.

To my mind, the nicest aspect of gardening is that no two gardens are the same. The way we select and use plants reflects our personalities and preferences. It is very important to have the

Annuals and perennials set the tone in this enchanting garden

flowers of our choice and the ones with which we feel comfortable.

The concept of choice makes gardening a glorious experiment. It allows us to garden by instinct and learn from our mistakes. If a plant is not doing well in a certain position, or doesn't suit the colour combination we are seeking, we should have the courage to move it. We should have confidence in our garden design and choose the annuals and perennials that we particularly appreciate.

It should be remembered that nature does not give its best results because one is in control of the garden. Spontaneity and naturalness are important factors, as surprise happenings give a garden feeling. And there is a paradox involved in creating a natural garden. All gardens were once wilderness but have been altered by a civilising, designing hand. There must be a balance between the natural and the cultivated. The Chinese have a saying: 'to tame the bird, let it fly free'. This means that to domesticate nature successfully, you should try to give up your desire to control all aspects of it.

With this philosophy in mind we can watch the garden as it unfolds, become aware of its fluid nature and use our intuition when cultivating it. We can fully appreciate the self-seeded annual which has appeared in the path, the uncontrolled climber spilling out of a tree or the groundcover which has set off in the wrong direction. These natural occurrences imbue a garden with charm and romance.

I have always felt that the transient nature of gardens should be encouraged rather than denied. The continual change allows us to enjoy particular, unique moments in the course of a year. Annuals and perennials accentuate that sense of change. They enable one to walk through the garden and observe what is happening as different plants appear through the seasons. One may discover annuals which have self-seeded from another part of the garden, or some long forgotten perennials. And while many gardeners prefer a short blaze of colour, I am prepared to wait for my garden to unfold gradually.

Because of their ability to reappear every year, perennials are the mainstay plants of an enchanting garden. As perennials multiply they may be divided and swapped with friends for other species or used to fill otherwise bare spaces in your garden.

Annuals are more versatile than perennials, and allow greater innovation. Planting annuals each year gives me the chance to experiment with colour and create a completely different tone in the garden. And self-seeding annuals will encourage the garden to develop its own distinctive and charming nature.

Annuals and perennials provide elegance through simplicity

An evocative planting of columbines

Combining for Effect

MOOD, tone and ambience are often insubstantial and variable characteristics. Yet it is often the ambience of a house or garden that affects us more than any particular, individual aspect.

Different architectural and decorating ideas are responsible for creating the mood of a house and this is also true of gardens. A number of factors contribute to garden enchantment, not the least of which is the combination of plants used. Successful combinations involve the correct use of colour and leaf texture.

PLANT COMBINATIONS

Plant combinations are very important to the structure of a garden. The strong forms and textures of different plants attract the eye's attention and hold it. Garden beds filled with plants of similar texture and form are always boring and unappealing. But garden beds filled with plants combining strong architectural shapes and fine or soft foliage prevent the garden looking flat. For example, dense, shrubby perennials with rich, dark green foliage stand out against a backdrop of fine, feathery foliage.

The use of different leaf textures provides essential form. The grouping and density of plants is also vital to the garden's structure. A garden with a formal framework can pull together the most disparate collection of plants and compensate for a host of planting deficiencies. But beds which have no framework need strong intrinsic form and texture to hold the eye. This means choosing plants which have some architectural value—plants with large, lacy or spiky leaves—or flowers grouped together to provide dramatic combinations.

A garden bed can rely entirely on foliage associations for effect. Placing different-shaped leaves together emphasises their diverse textures and shapes. And as you become more conscious of shapes and textures, you will find their

The large leaves of hostas provide strong architectural shapes

associations just as rewarding as colour combinations. Bold leaves, for example, look more pronounced when planted next to soft, fine leaves.

The swaying leaves of tall, ornamental grasses look elegant when planted among broad-leafed plants. The strap-like, ornamental grass leaves also provide a vertical emphasis in the garden. Blue fescue grass (*Festuca ovina 'Glauca'*) has outstanding powder blue foliage and will thrive in either cold or hot climates. It reaches a height of 30 cm.

The shiny brown foliage of brown sedge (*Carex buchananii*) produces a rare colour. Next to blue, white or yellow flowers the effect is exquisite. Brown sedge grass reaches a height of 60 cm, so it is a dramatic plant.

Lace-like leaves should be placed next to plain leaves. The deeply serrated leaves of the marguerite daisy (*Chrysanthemum frutescens*) have a softening effect on most plants and should be interspersed with plain foliage plants.

One does need to have many different plants for an eye-catching effect. For example, a border for a sunny pathway can be made to look stunning by incorporating three different types of plants. Standard white roses like 'Iceberg' will provide height and colour from spring until autumn. These could be underplanted with bearded irises which have strap-like leaves. Use the same colour, or tones of the same colour, for a stronger more unified effect. Next to the iris you should place a perennial with soft leaves like the Swan River daisy (*Brachycome iberidifolia*), meadow crane's bill (*Geranium pratense*), Iberian crane's bill (*Geranium ibericum*) or snow-

Combining for Effect

An interesting composition of tall flowers

in-summer (*Cerastium tomentosum*) to spill over the side of the path.

Spikes and spires

Spikes and spires are always enchanting. And in terms of garden architecture, it is effective to use foliage or flower heads which have a tall and vertical emphasis.

Many annuals and perennials have pretty, spire-like flowers and clumps of these placed randomly throughout garden beds create an interesting composition. Such a random placing of taller plants produces a natural effect in contrast with the traditional smooth change of flower and foliage height from the front to the back. Lower plants are not hidden, but framed between taller-growing ones.

Use these tall, spire-like flowers between structural plants like shrubs and roses. The architectural qualities of these tall flowers are like punctuation marks which cause you to stop and look.

The classic vertical plants featured in English cottage gardens and which always remind me of children's storybooks are foxgloves, hollyhocks and campanulas. While the tall flower spike of the foxglove can reach 2 m the hollyhock can do better still, reaching a height of 2.5 m. Grow foxgloves in dappled shade and an acid soil and hollyhocks in a sunny position with well-drained soil.

The tall flowers of *Campanula* species, which includes Canterbury bells (*Campanula medium*), are always impressive. Include *C. persicifolia* 'Sessiliflora', which reaches 1 m and has blue, bell-shaped, mid-summer blooms, and the giant bellflower *C. latifolia*, which is loved for its tubular blue flowers.

The pale-rose to red flowers of red valerian (*Centranthus ruber*) appear continuously throughout spring and summer. This hardy evergreen perennial has bluish green flowers and will grow in full sun or light shade. There is also a very pretty white-flowered form.

One of the nicest features that I

Foxgloves are exquisite vertical plants

The look in this garden is evocative and slightly dishevelled

remember about the Pyrenees is being able to walk through the tall flowerheads of lupins. Apart from their beautiful flower heads, lupins are excellent for the soil and are used in organic gardens as a green manure because of the nitrogen-fixing bacteria contained in their root nodules. They also have a wonderfully deep tap-root which, in the case of annual lupins, should be left in the soil to break down in order to add organic matter. Annual lupins grow through winter and their generous spikes of spring flowers appear in shades of blue, mauve, yellow and white.

The perennial lupin (*Lupinus polyphyllus* 'Russell Lupins') reaches a height of 1-2 m and is at its best in cold winter climates. Colours include maroon, gold, apricot, yellow, pink and shades of blue. Plant lupins in a sunny position and a medium-fertile, well-drained soil. One of their nice attributes is that they do not need excessive attention. Weak liquid feeding with a soluble fertiliser when the buds appear will promote larger flowers.

I don't know why purple loosestrife (*Lythrum salicaria*) isn't more popular. This perennial is invaluable for moist, badly drained soils. The early summer flower spikes reach a height of 1 m and completely cover the plant. You could combine it with white or pink goat's beard, which also like damp conditions.

The flowers of goat's beard (*Astilbe x arendsii*) are carried above the shining fern-like foliage and bring a soft, feathery tone with their plumes in spring. Plant goat's beard in dappled shade and keep the soil well-mulched, especially during the hot summer months. There are numerous named varieties.

Grey leaves can be used to brighten up or to tone down colour in the garden. Two superb plants with grey leaves and tall flower spikes are mullein (*Verbascum bombyciferum*) and *Salvia argentea*. Both plants have woolly, silver foliage and the felted leaves form a rosette from which

branching stems and flower spikes arise. Mullein has yellow flowers from mid-summer onwards and the clusters of sage-like white flowers of *Salvia argentea* appear around the same time. *Verbascum chaixii* reaches a height of 1 m and has yellow flowers with mauve eyes. The variety 'Album' bears spikes of white flowers which also have mauve eyes.

Acanthus mollis is more often grown for its large deep green leaves but the stately spikes of funnel-shaped, mauve and white flowers make a splendid show in summer. Place acanthus in sun or semi-shade.

Red hot pokers (*Kniphofia* species) and the foxtail lily (*Eremurus robustus*) are valued for their flowers—which appear on erect stems—and their strap-like leaves. Red hot pokers start flowering in summer and continue until autumn. There are many different cultivars and flower colours include red and yellow and combinations of these.

The foxtail lily is often thought of as a bulbous plant rather than as a perennial because of its strap-like leaves. These leaves die back during summer when it bears huge racemes of cup-shaped pink blooms.

I can't imagine a spring garden without the tall flowerheads of delphiniums. When planted in clumps they create a stunning sight. The stately flowerheads of the perennial *Delphinium elatum* 'Pacific Giant' can reach a height of 2 m. Colours are cream, white, pink and deep and light shades of blue or violet. *D. grandiflorum* is known as the butterfly or Chinese delphinium and has 4 cm wide flowers in white, blue, lilac and lavender.

The annual delphinium which is also commonly called larkspur (*Consolida ambigua* syn. *D. ajacis*) has tall, slender stems with erect racemes of lavender, blue, white and pink spring flowers. The fine, lacy foliage is invaluable in a garden bed.

An inspiring combination - Onopordum acanthium and white foxgloves

Colour Design

ALTHOUGH a successful garden is based on elements like design, texture and form, it is colour that provides the most immediate and enduring impression. Colour sets the tone of a garden and can even control the pace at which you walk through it. Shady green areas will make you want to slow down or even sit, while a brilliant planting at the end of a pathway will lure you towards it. Strong colours like yellow, red or orange stand out and advance towards you while blues, purples and greys tend to recede.

Colour affects people in different ways. Some gardeners prefer strong tones like yellows and reds to create an exuberant effect, while others tend towards more tranquil and relaxing colours like blue, pink and white.

A gardener should become aware how colours change in the morning and evening light. Even within the one colour there are different gradations. Shades of green foliage can be used to create contrasts between light and shadow. Leaf shapes, texture, size and surface sheen all help to enhance the effects of light. So one of the first rules to accept when working with colour is that the green of foliage is a colour just as much as any flower colour. Within the colour green itself there are pale yellow greens through to dark purplish greens. The first soft green, spring leaves will turn to a darker, summer green before they turn to yellow or red in autumn.

The famous Impressionist Claude Monet spent many hours painting in his garden at Giverny in France. Monet used plant colour to increase the effects of changes in time, season and weather. Monet demonstrated in his art an understanding of the almost magical ability of light to soften colour at certain times and create dazzling displays at others. In order to utilise the light of the setting sun, he planted rich orange, pink, gold and bronze wallflowers and tulips on the west side of the flower garden. He

Yellow and gold flowers have an intrinsic radiance

A bold colour theme can be inspiring

also used many clear blue and delicate salmon hues to convey the tonal feeling of mist softening the morning light. Monet placed plants with pastel hues in the distance behind brighter colours of the same tones in the foreground to produce the illusion of distance in the mist.

Unlike the static canvas of the artist, colour in the garden evolves and then fades as flowers die and leaves change colour. But this process lends itself to endless possibilities. My front garden in late winter and early spring is replete with blue forget-me-nots and yellow jonquils sitting above them. After a cold winter I find such colours warm and cheerful. As these die down, the garden colours will change to the pinks and whites of weigelas, old-fashioned roses, arum lilies, babies' tears, foxgloves, daisies, poppies and meadow rue. Blue reappears with columbines, species geraniums, campanulas, delphiniums, cornflowers and Jacob's ladder. Even within a season you will find that the colour can change dramatically in just one area of your garden.

The size of a garden will affect your colour choice. In small courtyards the colours chosen will usually relate to the colour of the house. A strong colour in the distance will foreshorten the sense of space, so arrange colour tones to become weaker in the distance. You may always add white or grey to most colour combinations as infillers and softeners.

As with all things in the garden, don't make colour co-ordination a chore. No matter how hard I try to colour co-ordinate parts of my garden, some other colour always creeps in. This year my red Flanders poppies self-seeded next to a clump of light purple and pink foxgloves in an area intended for shades of pink, white and blue. I sometimes wince as I walk past them but it doesn't bother me enough to remove them. I will, however, collect the Flanders poppy seeds when they ripen and place them in another area of the garden.

Monochromatic colour

If you like the idea of having only one colour throughout the garden, you should explore the use of monochromatic colour themes. Monochromatic colours are tints and shades of one colour. If you imagine a combination of maroon snapdragons, red and rose-coloured nicotiana and pale pink dianthus you will begin to understand the possibilities of such a scheme.

In reality there are no totally monochromatic gardens, as various shades of leaf green will always be part of the combination, but the presence of these shades is pleasant and will not detract from the dominant flower colours. In small gardens a monochromatic theme is not overpowering, while in a large space it can be very visually effective.

Analogous colour

An analogous colour theme makes use of neighbours on the colour wheel; any three colours found in sequence are said to comprise an analogous relationship. An example of such a relationship is yellow-green, yellow and yellow-orange.

To expand the possibilities of such a colour theme, you should include tints and shades of each of the three colours.

Complementary colour

Complementary colours are those which are the opposite to each other. Orange and blue are complementary, as are red and green. A stunning example of the use of complementary colours is orange calendulas set among blue daisies (*Felicia amelloides*) with a backdrop of dark blue delphiniums. Complementary colours intensify each other and colour schemes which utilise them are best confined to sections or pockets of the garden. They are powerful, vibrant combinations and look best when used with pure hues (rather than shades or tints) of the strong complementary colours. To tone down these colours you can use silver-foliaged plants and white flowers.

Pink and blue flowers contrast perfectly with dark green foliage

Polychromatic colour

For a carnival effect in the garden, try a polychromatic colour theme. This involves random combinations of any and every colour around the wheel, but take care as this can also look like the work of an inexperienced gardener. The best technique for a kaleidoscope of colour is to incorporate plenty of white. Colours tend to keep their own identities when they are surrounded by white and are less affected by neighbouring hues. Where space is limited, try using white vertically by employing tower-

Blocks of one colour can be used to create a directional effect

ing foxgloves, delphiniums or Canterbury bells. Grey variegated leaves may also be used to break up colours.

Blocks of Colour

Large blocks of a single colour can look particularly spectacular. For the most interesting effect, use just one type of plant. For example, a bed filled with lavender and surrounded by a box hedge can create a strong tone.

Blocks of one colour can also be used to create a directional effect. Line a pathway with a wide planting of, say, catmint (*Nepeta x faassenii*), lavender, daisies or irises.

Drifts of Colour

Drifts of one colour have a natural appearance and are often created by using bulbs, especially bluebells, daffodils and jonquils.

Annuals also produce delightful colour drifts. Forget-me-nots will reappear every year of their own accord to form a beautiful bed of pink, white or blue. They can be grown in the shade and are particularly handy for planting under trees.

Lovehearts (*Silene coeli-rosa*) form masses of flowers in shades of pink, red, white and blue. The intensity of flower colour is increased and the flowering period is actually prolonged when they are planted in areas of limited shade.

Foliage may also be used for drifts. *Lamium galeobdolon*, with its silver-splashed leaves, is ideal for areas under trees where it is difficult to get anything else to grow. In spring such areas will be lightened up even more by lamium's yellow flowers. Bugle weed (*Ajuga reptans*), or

An arresting composition in yellow and orange

Soft lavender and light blue flowers have a gentle, calming effect

one of its varieties, could also be used.

Colour themes

Using colour in the garden is probably the closest many of us ever get to painting. Plants may be treated as elements in a composition, but while a painting is one-dimensional a garden is full of living three-dimensional entities.

Once the structural plants like trees and shrubs have been chosen for the garden we can start 'painting' with annuals and perennials. The ultimate choice of colour is very personal. The colour range in your garden reflects your personality in much the same way as the colour of your clothes. The main point to remember is that colours should always blend with one another, and this is true whether you have only one or two colours through your garden or a variety of themes in different areas.

Blue

An all blue garden demands the viewer's consideration because of its unusual hues and the jewel-like quality of many of the flowers. There is something enchanting about a blue garden because it is quiet and restful while still being strong enough to attract attention. Blue is a cool colour available in many shades which are capable of creating a variety of effects. The brighter blues lift and brighten the garden while the softer lavenders and light blues have a more gentle, calming effect.

Light has a marked influence on the colour blue. Blue cornflowers or Chinese forget-me-nots produce a sharp, cheerful impression in the midday sun but, as the light fades in the evening, the effect is cooler and more mysterious.

Blue is always intensified by grey or silver leaves and white flowers. The quality of the blue can also be intensified by the correct juxtaposition of adjacent colours. Blue is perfect when placed next to yellow, as Monet demonstrated repeatedly. And blue is certainly brought to life by the addition of orange. Incorporate yellow into a blue theme by introducing daylilies, evening primrose, santolina, hypericum, wallflowers or lemon marguerite daisies. It is also possible to combine blue with pink, mauve and white. Such a combination could also incorporate a small amount of creamy yellow.

If you wish to expand the colour spectrum of a blue garden you should include shades of purple and violet. To this you could also add pink and a splash of lemon. Shady areas can be planted with forget-me-nots and purple honesty (*Lunaria annua*). Both plants will self-seed readily.

As already mentioned, blue is a colour that can readily be used by itself. A drift of bluebells or forget-me-nots is an exceptional sight. A mass planting of *Lobelia erinus* looks spectacular and provides a vivid contrast with softer shades of blue. Although short in stature and with small flowers, lobelia gives a vast amount of deep blue when in flower. The stems are slender, but when the plants are grown closely together they form a continuous colour border.

The *Campanula* species embraces nearly all the shades of blue. *C. portenschlagiana* has 1.75 cm wide, bell-shaped, deep blue flowers from summer to autumn which look outstanding against its heart-shaped foliage. This evergreen perennial reaches a height of only 15 cm but will spread to 45 cm. *C. poscharskyana* reaches a similar height and width and produces its star-shaped blue flowers in summer and autumn. Both species make excellent groundcovers.

Tall-growing perennial campanulas include *C. persicifolia*, which reaches 1 m and has bell-shaped, mid-summer blooms and the giant bellflower *(C. latifolia)* which is loved for its tubular purplish blue flowers. I can't imagine my summer garden without Canterbury bells (*Campanula medium*). The enormous bell-shaped flowers (4.5 cm long) never fail to impress me as they hang from the tall stem for up to

nine weeks in summer. This evergreen biennial will flower the following year if cut back to ground level when the flowers have finished.

An electrifying combination of yellow and blue flowers

The blue marguerite (*Felicia amelloides*), which is also known as the blue daisy will reward you with its flowers virtually all year round, especially in warm weather. The bright blue flowers have a prominent yellow centre and cover the 45 cm high evergreen bush. The foliage is aromatic. It creates an electrifying effect when planted in combination with yellow or orange marigolds.

Iberian crane's bill (*Geranium ibericum*) and meadow crane's bill (*Geranium pratense*) make spectacular groundcovers. They

A white garden will always attract attention

both have deeply cut, handsome leaves and look arresting when planted *en masse*, in tubs or as low-growing features in a border. Iberian crane's bill is an evergreen perennial with 2.5 cm wide violet-blue summer flowers. The large blue flowers of meadow crane's bill appear for weeks.

Blue-flowering annuals make fast-growing fillers and are all delightful in their own way. Bright green, lace-like foliage forms an attractive background to the pretty purple, light blue or mauve summer and autumn flowers of love-in-a-mist (*Nigella damascena*). When the flowers have finished the globe-shaped seed pods look most attractive. Other annuals could include pansies, especially the variety 'Shades of Blue'; blue cup flower (*Nierembergia hippomanica*), whose violet-blue flowers last through summer and into autumn and, of course, the very deep-blue petunias.

White

Keeping things simple can pay off, particularly when it comes to colour. Green has many associations and may signify freshness and regeneration. White is valued for its capacity to attract attention without being overpowering. A combination of the two creates a visually interesting and versatile effect, especially in summer. White flowers also bring the garden alive at night.

White is a safe colour that is bright and inoffensive. A garden filled with white foxgloves, delphiniums, roses, lilies, tree peonies, marguerite daisies, valerian and lupins will have a magical effect.

Combine white with silver and green

foliage and expand it into the shades of cream.

Green on green

Green is often overlooked as a garden colour. But the predominance of green in any garden is inevitable. In gardens where green is the main colour one must rely on compositions of foliage associations which use the texture and shape of different leaves to gain an effect. The more one considers the highly individual shapes of leaves the more important leaves become in your garden planning. Consider soft, lace-like leaves like those of bronze fennel set against bolder leaves like those of hostas and you will start to see the endless possibilities. A groundcover like lamium, which has silver-green leaves can lighten up an otherwise dark area and looks attractive when planted in shade next to the more solid leaves of bergenias or hostas.

When green is used as the dominant garden colour its appearance should not be dull. As you become more aware of shapes and textures you will find it as exciting to work with as any of the colours you have used in colour combinations.

Large flowerheads of lupins produce spectacular colour in spring borders

Silver and grey

Silver and grey are interesting because they are rather indeterminate colours. In fact, it is debatable whether they are colours at all, as they are not part of the colour spectrum. But the shimmering, almost ethereal tones of silver and grey plants offer many creative possibilities to the imaginative gardener.

Silver and grey plants are superb in a thematic garden or when used as accent plants. They will highlight dull corners, add light to a predominantly dark green

The silver leaves and yellow flowers of mullein contrast perfectly

They also retain moisture close to the leaf's surface and keep the tissues cool.

Silver and grey plants are thus perfect for the hot inland areas and foreshores of Australia. Many grey plants will thrive where other plants can't survive. Their use, however, is not limited to harsh areas as they do just as well or even better in good conditions.

When silver and grey are planted at the end of a border they create a sense of extended perspective. When planted among brightly coloured flowers they will tone down the effect of the colour. On the other hand, silver and grey plants will tone up dark colours. If you wish to use a great deal of silver and grey in the garden, I suggest that you are careful to choose plants with a marked variation in tone, texture and shape.

Grey plants are closely associated with herbs and are often used as the border for a herb garden. *Santolina*, lavender and *Senecio* 'Silver Dust' form ideal borders for Elizabethan knot gardens or formal herb gardens.

Interestingly, yellow seems to be the predominant flower colour of grey plants. But perfectionists with grey theme gardens generally remove the flower heads because they enjoy leaf texture and colour only. However, I love the combination of blue, lavender, purple and white flowers with grey. It is a soft, pleasing combination to which I will often add a small touch of pink.

Lavender deserves a place in any grey and silver garden because of its perfumed foliage. The many varieties also produce pretty spikes of lavender, blue, purple, white or pink flowers.

Cotton lavender (*Santolina chamaecyparissus*) is a low-growing shrubby perennial having finely dissected, aromatic leaves and yellow flowers in summer. Pinch out the young shoots to encourage bushy growth. It has been used for centuries in Europe as a border or hedging plant in knot and herb gardens.

garden bed and provide a feeling of freshness to well-established areas. In addition, many silver and grey plants are visible at night.

Silver and grey plants are well suited to the Australian climate. The majority of grey plants grow naturally in harsh conditions like shorelines, deserts and alpine areas. Many silver and grey foliage plants originally came from the coast of the Mediterranean but Australia has a rich variety of plants with these soft colours. After all, grey is a prominent colour in our landscape as Australian flora is always thought of as being more grey-blue than green.

The grey and silver appearance of plants is the result of a layer of white hairs on the leaf surface. The purpose of this layer is to reduce water loss as the hairs reflect the harsh rays of the sun.

Flowers for a Yellow or Gold Colour Theme

Achillea filipendula (yarrow)
Achillea tomentosa (yarrow)
Alstroemeria aurea (Peruvian lily)
Aquilegia hybrids (columbine)
Aurinia saxatilis (yellow alyssum)
Chrysanthemum frutescans (Marguerite daisy)
Chrysanthemum morifolium (perennial chrysanthemum)
Dahlia hybrids (bedding dahlias)
Doronicum plantagineum (leopard's bane)
Gazania x hybrida
Hedychium flavum (ginger lily)
Helenium autumnale (sneeze weed)
Helianthemum nummularium (sun rose)
Hemerocallis hybrids (daylily)
Hibbertia serpyllifolia (Guinea flower)
Kniphofia hybrids (red hot poker)
Oenothera biennis (evening primrose)
Paeonia lutea (yellow peony)
Polyanthus species (polyanthus)
Rudbeckia hybrids (rudbeckia)
Santolina chamaecyparissus (cotton lavender)
Solidago canadensis (golden rod)

Flowers for a White Garden Theme

Plants in this list include varieties of flowers in the colour range from white to cream.

Acanthus mollis (bear's breeches)
Achillea millefolium (yarrow)
Alcea rosea (hollyhock)
Alstroemeria aurea (Peruvian lily)
Anemone blanda (woodland anemone)
Anemone x hybrida (windflower)
Anthemis nobilis (flowering chamomile)
Aquilegia vulgaris (columbines)
Arabis albida (rock cress)
Arenaria montana (sandwort)
Artemisia lactiflora (Chinese mugwort)
Aster novi-belgii (Michaelmas daisy)
Astilbe x arendsii (goat's beard)
Campanula medium (Canterbury bells)
Campanula rotundifolia 'Alba' (English harebell)
Cerastium tomentosum (snow-in-summer)
Chrysanthemum frutescans (Marguerite daisy)
Chrysanthemum morifolium (perennial chrysanthemum)
Chrysanthemum parthenium (feverfew)
Chrysanthemum superbum (shasta daisy)
Convallaria majalis (lily-of-the-valley)
Dahlia hybrids (bedding dahlias)
Delphinium elatum 'Pacific Giant' (delphiniums)
Dianthus caryophyllus (carnation)
Dictamnus albus (burning bush)
Digitalis purpurea (foxglove)
Erigeron karvinskianus (babies' tears)
Gazania x hybrida (gazania)
Gypsophila paniculata (baby's breath)
Gypsophila repens (fairy grass)
Helleborus corsicus (Corsican hellebore)
Helleborus niger (Christmas rose)
Hemerocallis hybrids (daylily)
Hosta plantaginea (plantain lily)
Lupinus hartwigii (lupins)
Lychnis coronaria 'Alba' (rose campion)
Paeonia lactiflora (Chinese peony)
Papaver orientale (oriental poppy)
Pelargonium x domesticum (regal pelargonium)
Pelargonium x hortorum (zonal geranium)
Penstemon hybrids (penstemon)
Phlox paniculata (perennial phlox)
Phlox subulata (alpine phlox)
Polyanthus species (polyanthus)
Polygonatum multifolium (Solomon's seal)
Polygonum bistorta (polygonum)
Primula species (primula)
Romneya coulteri (romneya)
Stokesia laevis (Stoke's aster)
Thymus serpyllum (wild or creeping thyme)
Verbena x hybrida (verbena)
Viola odorata (sweet violet)

A strong image of dark pink and rich blue

There is an abundance of silver and grey perennials. Thrift, (*Armeria maritima*), which forms a low, cushion-like carpet and has flowers varying from white to crimson, is excellent for the edge of an herbaceous border. Wormwood (*Artemisia absinthium*), a shrubby perennial, will give structure to a border or will make a splendid low hedge. It has deeply dissected leaves covered in fine, silky hairs which give the whole plant a silvery sheen. *Eryngium maritimum* is an eye-catching plant with a thistle-like appearance. Its flowers, stems and leaves have a silvery-blue hue.

Lamb's ears (*Stachys byzantina*), which is known more widely under its previous name *S. lanata*, is one of my favourite perennials. Its large, thick, silvery-grey leaves are heavily felted. During summer its purple flowers appear on tall spikes.

Mullein (*Verbascum bombyciferum*) is a spectacular plant for the back of a garden bed. Its giant grey-white leaves (often 50 cm long) have a felted appearance. A biennial, it reaches a height of 2 m and a width of 70 cm.

Rose campion (*Lychnis coronaria*) is a self-seeding perennial which, once established, will pop up throughout the garden in unexpected places. The grey leaves and stems have a flannel-like appearance. The bright-cerise flowers appear in early summer. 'Alba' is a white variety and the white flowers of 'Ocellata' have a pink eye.

Flannel flower (*Actinotus helianthi*) is one of the most stunning grey native plants. The soft, silver leaves and white flowers appear in spring and summer. It has the reputation of being difficult to grow but success is assured when it is given

FLOWERS FOR A BLUE COLOUR THEME

Plants in this list include colours from blue and violet to lavender and bluish purple.

Aconitum napellus (monkshood)
Anemone blanda (woodland anemone)
Aquilegia flabellata (columbine)
Aquilegia vulgaris (columbine)
Aster novi-belgii (Michaelmas daisy)
Brachycome multifida (Swan River daisy)
Brunnera macrophylla (summer forget-me-not)
Campanula isophylla (Italian bellflower)
Campanula medium (Canterbury bells)
Campanula persicifolia 'Sessiliflora' (peach-leaved campanula)
Campanula portenschlagiana (campanula)
Campanula rotundifolia (English harebell)
Delphinium species (delphinium)
Echinops ritro (globe thistle)
Echium fastuosum (viper's bugloss)
Felicia amelloides (blue marguerite)
Gentiana acaulis (gentian)
Geranium pratense (meadow crane's bill)
Houstonia caerulea (blue cushion)
Limonium latifolium (perennial statice)
Lupinus x hybrida (lupins)
Meconopsis betonicifolia (Himalayan blue poppy)
Phlox species (phlox)
Platycodon grandiflorum (balloon flower)
Primula species (primulas)
Salvia farinacea (blue sage)
Stokesia laevis (Stoke's aster)
Thalictrum dipterocarpum (lavender shower)
Thymus species (thyme)
Verbena x hybrida (verbena)
Veronica spicata (speedwell)
Viola odorata (sweet violet)

FLOWERS FOR A RED COLOUR THEME

Flowers in this list include crimson, burgundy and dark pink.

Achillea millefolium 'Cerise Queen' (yarrow)
Anemone x hybrida (Japanese anemone)
Astilbe x arendsii (goat's beard)
Centranthus ruber (red valerian)
Chrysanthemum coccineum (red pyrethrum)
Chrysanthemum morifolium (perennial chrysanthemum)
Dahlia hybrids (bedding dahlias)
Dianthus caryophyllus (carnation)
Gazania x hybrida (gazania)
Geum quellyon (scarlet avens)
Hemerocallis hybrids (day lily)
Heuchera sanguinea (coral bells)
Kniphofia hybrids (red hot poker)
Lychnis coronaria (rose campion)
Paeonia lactiflora (Chinese peony)
Papaver orientale (oriental poppy)
Pelargonium x domesticum (regal pelargonium)
Pelargonium x hortorum (zonal geranium)
Penstemon hybrids (penstemon)
Phlox paniculata (perennial phlox)
Polyanthus species (polyanthus)
Verbena x hybrida (verbena)

FLOWERS FOR A PINK COLOUR THEME

Alcea rosea (hollyhock)
Anemone blanda (woodland anemone)
Anemone x hybrida (windflower)
Aster novi-belgii (Michaelmas daisy)
Astilbe rivularis (goat's beard)
Bellis perennis (English daisy)
Bergenia cordifolia (Norwegian snow)
Campanula medium (Canterbury bells)
Chrysanthemum frutescans (Marguerite daisy)
Delphinium species (delphiniums)
Dianthus species (cottage pinks)
Digitalis purpurea (foxgloves)
Erigeron karvinskianus (babies' tears)
Lupinus hartwegii (lupin)
Papaver orientale (oriental poppy)
Penstemon gloxinoides (penstemon)
Phlox species (phlox)
Saxifraga umbrosa (London pride)
Statice species (statice)
Thymus species (thyme)

full sun and perfect drainage.

Yellow and gold

Yellow and gold lighten a garden, drawing the eye to their intrinsic radiance. Yellow is a cheerful colour as it suggests fields before the harvest, spring primroses and daffodils.

Unfortunately, yellow is not an easy colour to use in the garden. Changing light can affect yellow more than any other colour. In spring before the sun is too bright it always looks fresh, but in summer it can take on brassy tones. In the shade, however, it will look good throughout the year.

Yellow combines well with scarlet and orange shades. The orange and scarlet flowers will dominate the scene and prevent the yellow from becoming too harsh in the sun. You can combine scarlet and orange nasturtiums, daylilies, dahlias, snapdragons, wallflowers and lilies with yellow pansies, achilleas, sunflowers, pot marigolds, evening primroses, euphorbia and Californian poppies.

Yellow and blue is a nice combination. Try yellow daylilies and blue lupins or yellow pot marigolds and blue delphiniums. A yellow and blue combination can also be used with purple, but care is needed as too much purple is overpowering when used with yellow. Blue and yellow combinations can be mixed successfully with white, and these colours are offset by the green of the leaves.

One usually uses white vertical plants to co-ordinate or lighten an assortment of colours and as accent plants, but light yellow or cream vertical plants have an ethereal effect. You should use cream foxgloves, mulleins, delphiniums or lupins.

Place grey-leafed plants among yellow ones for a lightening effect. Fortunately many grey-leafed plants like chamaecyparissus and mulleins have yellow flowers. Make sure there is still plenty of green among the grey and yellow especially during summer.

The pot marigold (*Calendula officinalis*) brings a real splash of colour to a gold garden because of its bright and showy yellow or orange flowers. If the seeds are allowed to ripen on the flower and fall, they will germinate the following season. Another stunning gold-flowering annual that will reappear the following year is the Californian poppy (*Eschscholzia californica*).

Pink

Pink is a versatile garden colour but has the tendency to look bland if used on its own. Soft pastel shades like pink need to be darkened with brighter colours and look especially good with colours of the same range. For instance, maroon combines well with various shades of pink. To this combination you might add a touch of white for an enlivening effect.

A colour theme of pink, blue, white and maroon is most pleasant. Maroon adds depth to the combination and is highlighted simultaneously by the pink. Instead of maroon you could always use a touch of purple to emphasise the blue.

Shades of red

The really brave—or the really extrovert—may wish to try a red theme. Red is not a particularly peaceful colour and is one of the most difficult colours to combine with other colours. But it certainly adds a sense of drama to a garden. A pure red garden bed is fun if you have the space, but make sure that other areas of your garden are in relaxing colours so that you are able to retreat to them when necessary.

I find scarlet-red flowers harder to combine than maroon reds. Scarlet flowers fit in best with shades of orange and yellow or may also be used with blue and white. Red Flanders or Oriental poppies against blue delphiniums or lupins create a bold effect. On the other hand, white can have a softening effect near scarlet reds, but when used with scarlet-red and blue it has a crisp, refreshing look. In large areas you will be able to combine scarlet and purple.

Very dark, bluish reds or shades of maroon are much easier to work into the garden than scarlet reds and even look good next to pinks. Pink and red sweet Williams mixed with a little white create a delightful scene.

One of the most appealing ways to use red is as an isolated accent. It will inject life into a bed and can be separated from other colours by the clever use of white.

For a stunning effect in large gardens plant a meadow of Flanders poppies (*Papaver rhoeas*) instead of a lawn. Success with Flanders poppies depends upon getting them established initially, as the soil must be fine and make contact with the seeds. These hardy poppies will self-seed each year and flower during spring and into summer to produce a really arresting red carpet.

Few flowers grow as readily, flower as profusely, and have such attractive foliage and charming flowers as cosmos. *Cosmos* 'Red Dazzler' looks wonderful when planted *en masse* or when combined with blue and white flowers.

Red oriental poppies (*Papaver orientale*) and rose campion (*Lychnis coronaria*) grow well in cool and temperate climates. The single, bright, crimson-red flowers of rose campion are tempered by its contrasting silver-grey stems and leaves.

Red valerian (*Centranthus ruber*) is an herbaceous perennial which grows pleasantly bushy and requires little attention apart from the cutting back of spent flowers. Plant it in dry situations where other plants find it difficult to grow.

Scarlet poppies combine perfectly with yellow and orange columbines

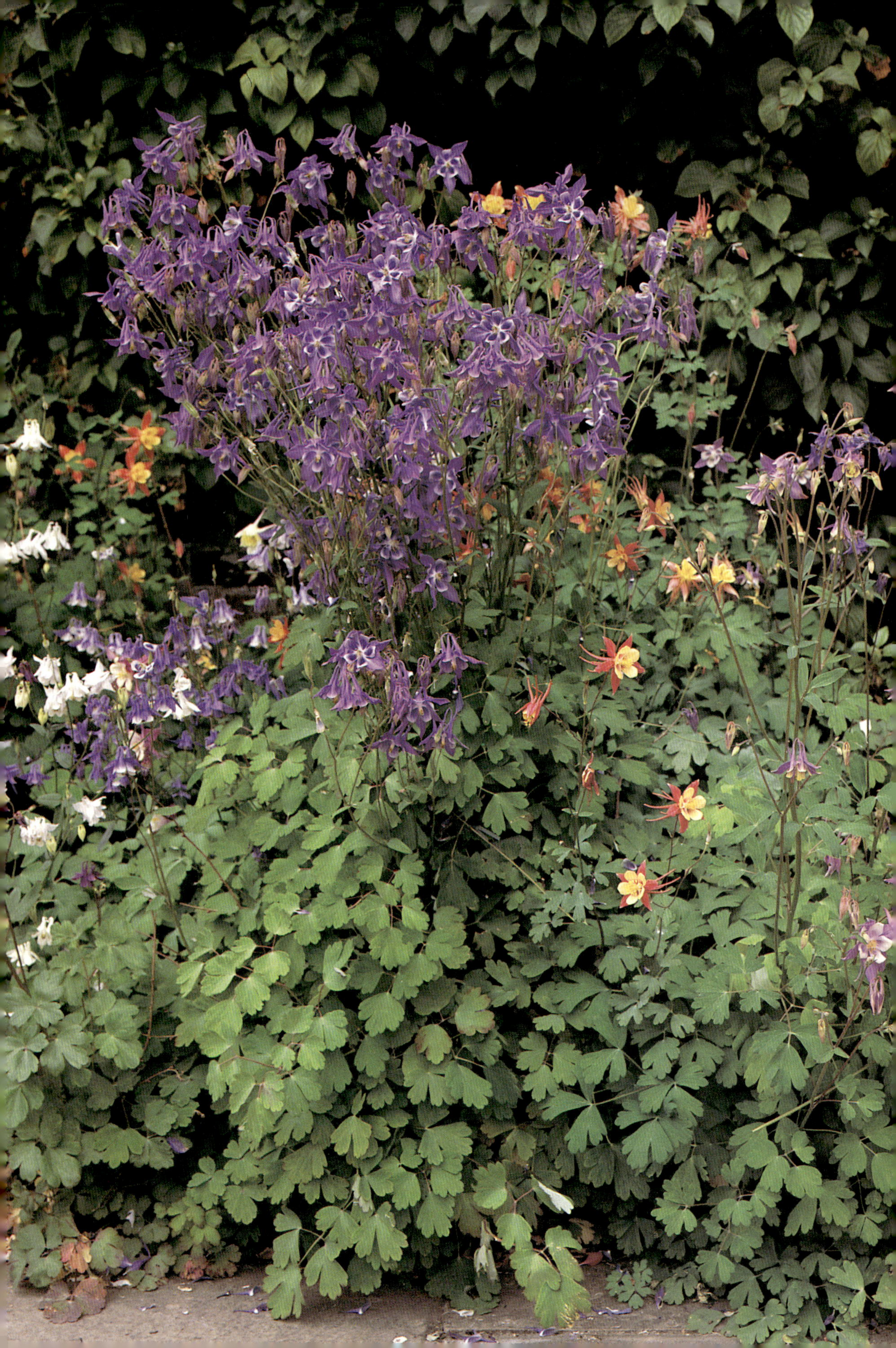

The Perennial Border

PERENNIAL gardening has a long and interesting history. The universal fascination with perennials has found its highest form of expression in the art of creating perennial borders.

Perennials are usually grown in herbaceous or mixed borders. A purely herbaceous border contains perennials only, while a mixed one supports annuals and perennials as well as bulbs, roses and shrubs. Climbers may be allowed to climb up, twine around and dangle from background trees. Shrubs in the border can physically support the arrangement, providing background and structure as well as lengthening the period of attraction.

A mixed border will create interest in the same spot throughout the year by reflecting the changing seasons. A mixed border will often have a more natural appearance and if you plant self-seeding annuals the border will soon take on a soft, romantic look rather than make an obvious statement.

A perennial border can be used to line a pathway, be planted beside a hedge or be placed against the wall of a house. If the border is lining a pathway or is capable of being viewed from both sides, then it should be designed accordingly, with tall-growing perennials in the middle of the bed and lower-growing plants on each side to give a tapering effect.

If the border is set against a hedge or wall, then tall plants should be used as background plantings with lower-growing ones being placed in order of decreasing height towards the front. Having said this, I find that several groups of taller plants placed randomly in the middle of the border create a more natural effect than a smooth change of height from the front to the back. Lower-growing plants need not be hidden, but framed between taller-growing ones. Remember that if changes in height are too abrupt the border will look artificial.

The rich colours of columbines provide the foundation of this early spring border

A romantic and relaxing perennial garden

It is worthwhile taking time to plan the border before you plant, as this will produce a cohesive design and ensure flower colour over a longer period. Don't think of plants in isolation, but instead create a picture in your mind of colour, texture and structure. A seasonal border will give a spectacular display, but if you decide on such a border, you must be willing to have fewer flowers for the rest of the season.

For a longer duration of colour, choose a continuous succession of blooms in which new flowers appear as others fade. Although this may reduce the visual impact of the overall garden colour, it will reveal the forms of the plants more clearly. Don't consider flower colour only, as foliage can create different interest and colour through the seasons. In all successful borders there is a harmonious balance of flowers and foliage.

Important design characteristics to keep in mind are colour, spread, form, texture and flowering time. The most interesting borders are comprised of a combination of plant forms. There are six basic shapes in which most perennials grow; rounded, vertical, open, upright, spreading and prostrate.

Flower forms also play a large part in the bed. Bear in mind that a garden bed filled mainly with daisy-like flowers, for example, may look flat and uninteresting. Try to include mixtures by using flowers with bell-shaped blooms like campanulas and penstemons, spherical peonies, spurred columbines, trumpet-like daylilies and frilly-flowered dianthus.

It is undoubtledly true that the design of a perennial garden achieves its impact from the combination of plants used. An important factor in plant combination is texture.

A variety of leaf and flower shapes enhances this border

Plant texture refers to the appearance of the plant. Plants with large, bold leaves like hostas are considered to be coarsely textured while plants with finely dissected, lacy leaves like lavender shower or marguerite daisies are considered to be finely textured. It is the mixture of different textures in a garden that will give it charm and create interest.

Texture can also be used in the garden to create spatial illusions. Coarsely textured plants always appear closer to the viewer than finely textured plants. In small gardens it is advisable to use a large number of finely textured plants to make the garden appear larger.

The use of strap-like leaves also provides interest in a garden border. Plants with such leaves could include daylilies and irises, which look lovely when planted in drifts.

Another design consideration is the appearance of the garden from indoors. If you spend a lot of time indoors, try to design the garden so it will look just as good from inside the house as outside.

When you have made your plant selection, plant in clumps and drift one mass into the other. Try not to plant in straight rows, unless you want a formal effect. Two or three perennials of the same type may be planted together. The overall effect of the border is enhanced when there are repeated groupings of plants placed at intervals. This will ensure a bold and visually arresting design.

A common mistake when planting out a new garden is to overplant. The majority of perennials spread every year and this should be taken into consideration from the outset. Although the garden bed may look bare to start with, it will not be long before it is full. Plants which have been given room to grow always look healthier than those which have been planted too closely together.

THE PERRENNIAL BORDER 41

> *The visual quality of this border can be attributed to the combination of plants used*

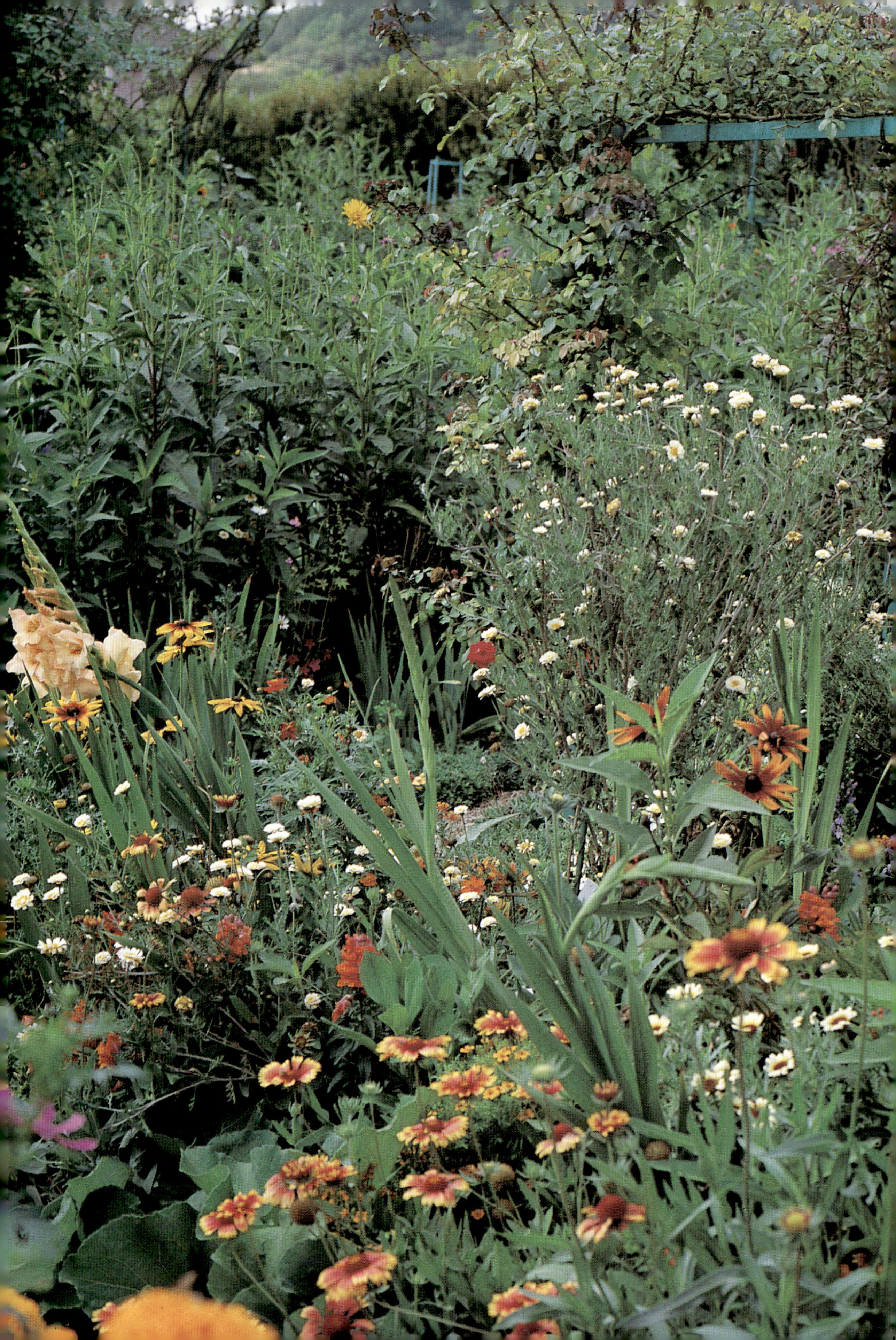

The Versatile Annual

UNFORTUNATELY the word 'annual' produces images of brightly coloured flowers planted predictably in rows. I always feel that this is unfortunate because annuals are actually very versatile plants which can be used to provide colour and interest in many situations. Their versatility enables them to be interplanted with perennials or spread in eye-catching drifts throughout the garden.

Annuals will contribute colour quickly in a range that can be bold or subtle according to your garden theme. They are especially suitable for use in new garden beds to cover bare earth and prevent weed growth.

I often think of annuals as infills for those times in your garden when extra colour is needed or when other plants are not sufficiently developed to provide interest in their own right. I always like to plant new annuals each season. This allows me the opportunity to play with colour in the garden, an opportunity not open to me with the structural, permanent plants.

Annuals create an enchanting effect and fit into the scheme of the garden in a natural way when planted informally. Plant them in drifts under trees or in clumps throughout the garden. Merge the clumps with neighbouring plants as this will ensure the covering of the earth and will give the garden a more unified appearance.

Annuals look good when used formally to line a path or surround a garden bed, especially if the planting behind them is informal. They can also be used as border plants around garden beds while slower-growing hedges or border plants mature.

In addition to the flowers of annuals, you should consider the leaf colour and texture of both the annuals themselves and the surrounding plants. Try to combine lacy leaves with bold ones, or jagged leaves with plain ones. This will add interest to the garden even before

The merging of annuals and perennials unifies this garden

A garden bed replete with self-seeding annuals

the flowers appear.

The term 'annual' refers to plants which grow from seeds, produce flowers and seeds and then die within a period of one year. My favourite annuals are the old-fashioned types with the ability to self-seed the following year. Flowers like forget-me-nots, love-in-a-mist and Queen Anne's lace will never fail you, and it is such simple flowers that produce a tone of enchantment in a garden. When used randomly they will soften the rigidity of a formal layout and extend the impression of a freer planting.

The forget-me-not has always been a much loved flower. It was a favourite of Henry IV, who made it his emblem while in exile. It is also the state flower of Alaska. On a more romantic note, there is the legend of the knight and the maiden who were walking near a lake when the maiden noticed some beautiful little flowers on a small island some distance from the shore. When the maiden expressed a desire to have some of these flowers, the knight swam to the island to gather them. While returning with the flowers his strength failed and, realising he would not reach the shore, he threw the flowers at the maiden's feet and cried 'forget-me-not' before sinking into the water. Such legends account for why, in the language of flowers, the forget-me-not signifies true love.

Forget-me-nots flower in spring but there is usually the odd flower around during summer and autumn. Apart from blue, they are also available in pink and white. Their greatest value is their ability to flower in sun or shade and they provide an attractive groundcover under shrubs. Blue forget-me-nots are outstanding when

Foxgloves create a sense of height in this annual and perennial garden

planted with yellow jonquils or daffodils. In shady areas they combine well with white or purple honesty. Although they have a very free self-seeding habit they are not difficult to remove when necessary.

Love-in-a-mist (*Nigella damascena*) and red campion (*Silene dioica*)—which is actually a perennial—are invaluable self-seeding plants. Red campion deserves to be as popular as the forget-me-not because it will thrive in sun or semi-shade. It is ideal for oversowing bulbs or planting in a cottage garden border with cosmos and salvia.

Although love-in-a-mist prefers full sun, I find that it performs nearly as well in partial shade. It is grown for its attractive flowers which float on a sea of dainty fern-like foliage. The seed pods can be dried for floral arrangements. The two varieties are 'Miss Jekyll', which is completely blue and 'Persian Jewels', which is a mixture of blue, pink and white.

There are some delightful blue flowering annuals. The well-known cornflowers are a must for every garden. The small forget-me-not-like flowers of *Anchusa capensis* 'Blue Bird' are a very clear blue. This hardy plant bears its flowers in early summer. The flowers of *Cynoglossum* are very similar.

Another flowering annual with intense blue flowers which is sometimes overlooked is the Californian bluebell (*Phacelia campanularia*). The deep green leaves of this fast-growing, bushy annual offset the bell-shaped flowers which appear in summer and early autumn.

While not being a lover of petunias, I admit to a fondness for the dark blue variety. Tucked in clumps at the front of the border or planted in terracotta pots, their effect can be quite stunning. If you want to be really bold, combine them with yellow calendulas or marigolds.

Spider flower (*Cleome hasslerana* syn. *C. spinosa*) is very useful for filling space at the back of a border. This bushy annual reaches a height of 1.2 m and the rose-pink or white flowers appear in summer. Combine spider flower with Queen Anne's lace and cosmos. Cosmos is available with pink or white flowers and the dainty heads of white Queen Anne's lace lend a delicate appearance to the garden. Both these self-seed yearly.

To add to the above combination do not forget blue, white or purple salvia (*Salvia farinacea*). The tall flower spikes last through summer and into autumn.

The clouds of tiny, white summer to autumn flowers of *Gypsophila elegans* look magical in a garden bed. Sow the seeds of this fast growing annual wherever it is to grow.

Green flowers are rare but when they are used in the garden they create a cool feeling and tone down the effect of brighter colours. Interesting green-flowering annuals include *Zinnia elegans* 'Envy', which reaches a height of 90 cm; bells of Ireland (*Molucella laevis*), which has tall spikes of

---

CHECKLIST FOR GROWING ANNUALS

- Don't plant seedlings too close together. Give plants enough room to reach their full size and you'll receive more flowers. However, you will find you can usually plant them at half the distance apart recommended on the packet.

- Plant sun-loving annuals in the sun only and shade-lovers in the shade or the plants will never actually achieve their full potential.

- Make sure the soil is rich and healthy before planting. Compost or manure can be dug into the soil or used as a mulch.

- Don't plant too early in spring as the soil is colder than the air temperature and seeds won't germinate.

- Avoid planting in straight rows. Plant in drifts or in clumps instead to produce a more informal tone.

green, open, bell-shaped flowers and lime green, flowering tobacco (*Nicotiana alata* 'Lime Green'). *N. alata* is a perennial but is usually treated as an annual.

One of my favourite annuals is lisianthus or prairie gentian (*Eustoma grandiflora*). The exquisite 50 mm wide blue, pink, rose or white flowers are bell-shaped. The foliage is pale green. For best results plant lisianthus in well-drained soil which has had lime added. Cut back after the first flush of flowers and you will be rewarded with more. Clumps of 5 or 6 are very eye-catching.

Pansies and heartsease are invaluable for edging pathways and both will tolerate some shade. Did you know that the more often you pick pansies the more flowers they will produce? For an exquisite effect combine black pansies with blue lobelias and blue or white pansies.

Lovehearts (*Silene coeli-rosa*) are shade-lovers which look marvellous when planted in large drifts under trees. Shade will deepen the colour and prolong the flowering period. Flower colours include mauve, blue and pastel pink. They are extremely easy to cultivate, so simply scatter the seeds where they are to grow and flowers will appear 12 weeks later. Plant them in all seasons except winter in tropical climates, and in spring and summer throughout the rest of Australia.

While on the subject of shade, honesty (*Lunaria annua*), which is available in white or purple, is extremely hardy and often thrives where nothing else will grow. The 'lunar' part of its Latin name refers to the moon-like, silvery white, flat seed pods which can be dried and used for indoor

Self-seeding heartsease, forget-me-nots and foxgloves form casual associations

decoration. But remember to leave some on the plant so it will reappear the following year. Its height and its slightly bushy habit make it a good infill plant for areas where it is difficult to grow other plants.

Wishbone flower (*Torenia fournieri*) has always been a cottage garden favourite. The pretty flower looks like a small, deep blue snapdragon with a pale centre. The leaves are a bronzy green.

Pincushion flower (*Scabiosa atropurpurea*) has always been a great favourite for bouquets and will thrive and even self-seed in dry soil and a sunny position. The colour range of the large pincushion-like flowers is most attractive, encompassing shades of white, blue and purple.

Larkspurs (*Delphinium ajacis*) reach a height of 1 m and will grow in full sun or partial shade. These annual delphiniums have deeply divided leaves and blue, pink, violet or white flowers with a pronounced spur.

Plant stocks (*Mathiola incana*) near a window or in a balcony container so their sweet perfume and subtle colours can be appreciated. The tall flower stalks will last for several weeks when picked. They are virtually trouble-free as long as they are given ample summer water.

Self-seeding annuals

Many annuals have the capability to shed their seeds throughout the garden and flowers will emerge the next year in the most unexpected places. Allowing plants to do this gives your garden a sense of intrigue and interest, as garden 'pictures' will appear spontaneously. Listed below are a selection of annuals which readily self-seed:

Ammi majus, Cynoglossum amabile, Eschscholzia californica , Impatiens wallerana, Lunaria annua, Myosotis sylvatica, Nicotiana sylvestris, Nigella damascena, Papaver species, *Primula malacoides, Scabiosa atropurpurea, Silene dioica, Tropaeolum majus, Silene coeli-rosa* syn. *Viscaria* species, *Viola tricolor*

This bold mixture of annuals and perennials produces an unusual summer colour scheme

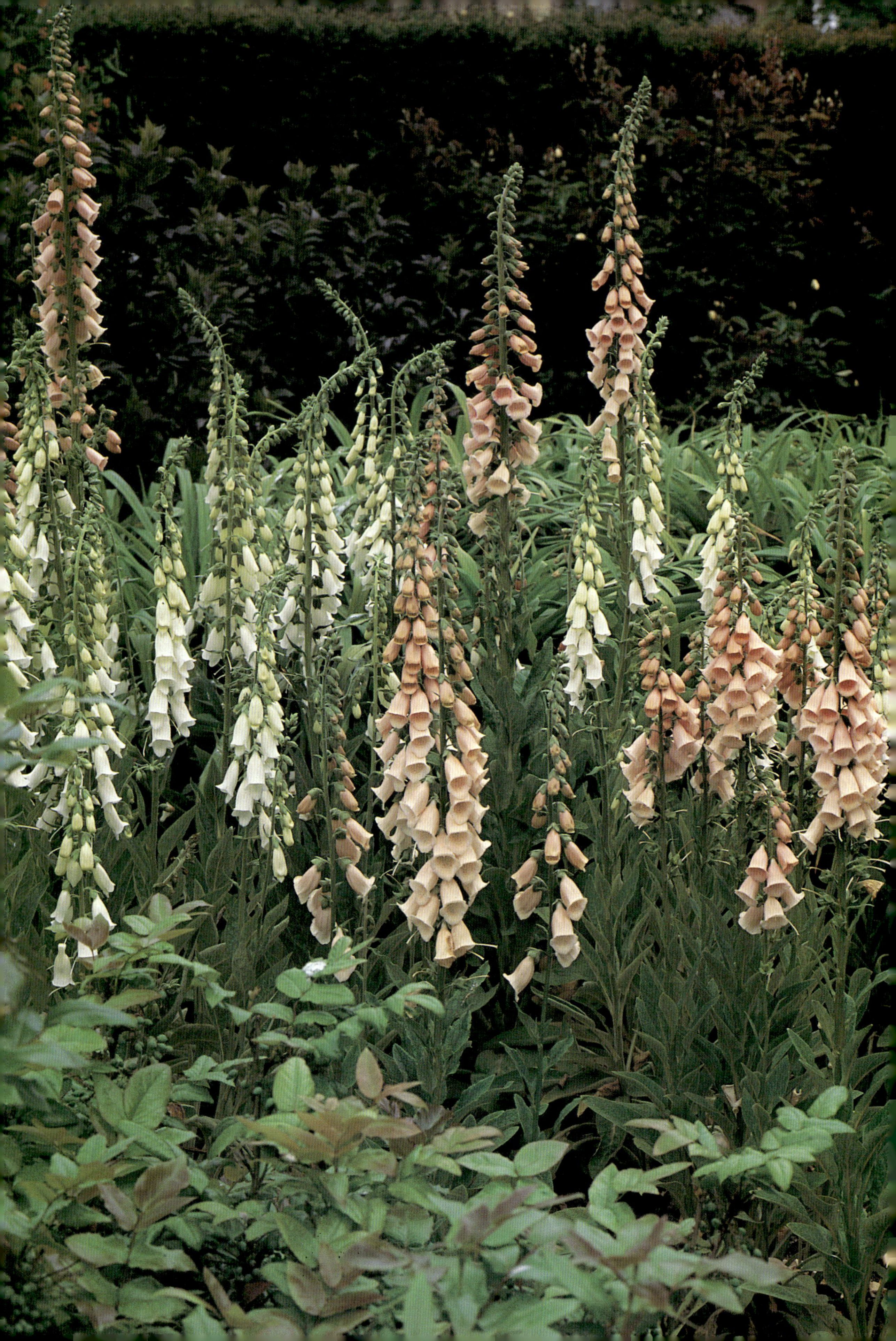

The Natural Garden

THE love of gardens and flowers is one of the most enduring of human interests. It finds expression in many ways—in poetry and painting as well as in the creation of gardens as sanctuaries of tranquillity and beauty.

This widespread, almost universal, interest in gardens is not surprising. After all, gardens are about life. And they offer us our own space to create the feeling we want around us. These days, many gardeners wish to encourage the wilder tendencies inherent in nature and oversee a garden which, once planted, will largely happen by itself.

The concept of a 'natural' garden is not new, of course, but it is one which is being progressively refined and modified in the late twentieth century. Many earlier garden designers have contributed to the popularity of natural gardens. One of the most famous designers associated with this approach, Gertrude Jekyll, developed her ideas in the nineteenth century. Born in 1843, her work exhibited a tasteful blend of the formal and informal. Her main aim and genius was to provide colour throughout the year, as well as the capacity of a garden to produce the right balance of colour, form and texture to match new architectural schemes.

Jekyll worked closely with Sir Edward Lutyens, an architect with a feeling for the natural disposition of plants in town and country gardens, and her work reflected simple elements of the countryside. Jekyll's own carefully designed garden at Munstead in Surrey was sheltered by trees such as mountain ash (*Sorbus aucuparia*), silver birch (*Betula pendula*), oak (*Quercus* species), beech (*Fagus* species) and yew (*Taxus baccata*). The dark yew hedges contrasted with and offset the softer colours of her herbaceous borders. Jekyll lived to 89 and in her last years failing eyesight

Foxgloves are perfect plants for natural gardens because of their capacity to self-seed

meant that eventually she could appreciate only the perfumes and textures of plants in her beautiful garden.

Vita Sackville-West was another lover of the natural approach and this is reflected in the garden she and her husband Harold Nicolson developed at Sissinghurst, Kent, between 1930 and 1961. Vita Sackville-West opposed the formal tidiness of gardens. She designed patchworks of walled or yew-hedged compartments which were laid out by her husband. Plants were raised in casual associations and seedlings were encouraged to grow wherever they sprang up.

The style of this informal cottage garden is relaxed but practical

It may sound paradoxical, but to achieve a natural garden much thought should go into garden design and the selection of trees, shrubs and plants. But this thought should be directed towards encouraging nature rather than imposing the narrow will and sense of order of the gardener. Things should be allowed to happen rather than being completely controlled. I feel very strongly that one should observe the garden and its changes to gain a sense of the spirit of the place before intervening.

A garden created according to these principles will have an informal appearance, and this informality will create an atmosphere of tranquillity, even intrigue, as surprising combinations and effects become apparent. The central notion of a natural garden is that, by using the right plant material, the garden will tend to look after itself and require the minimum of maintenance. Once the garden is planted it should be a place you enjoy, not one that needs every weekend to keep it in order. The weekends should be spent sitting in the garden or entertaining in it. The garden should be a place where one can relax in a natural setting.

A natural garden is one in which there is a profusion of groundcovers, bulbs, annuals and perennials. There should be no bare earth in sight. Annuals and perennials are allowed to self-seed yearly and are not planted in straight lines but in drifts to create an informal look. Plants appear by themselves in unexpected places. There are patches of self-sown columbines and foxgloves, or wandering groundcovers that have set off in unexpected directions. Climbers are allowed to wander through trees and shrubs to invest the garden with a romantic feeling. The long stems twining through trees or hanging from them create a softening effect.

Garden design is a very individual thing which varies with the size of the land and the climate. But there are essential rules to be followed if you want to have a natural garden.

As already mentioned, allowing your annuals and perennials to self-seed is an important aspect of the natural garden. Many gardening books warn of plants seeding throughout the garden and advise that they should be uprooted or have the seedheads cut off before this happens. But these procedures are usually unnecessary, as nature has its own way of inhibiting the proliferation of plants. Many seeds will fall in places that are too dry or shady to allow germination.

A pathway lined with a variety of self-seeding plants

Try to disturb the soil as little as possible to facilitate germination. This may be difficult when the garden is young because weeds are prone to appear before the soil is completely covered with perennials and groundcovers. Carefully pull out any weeds by hand, and ensure that tiny seedlings are not disturbed. If the garden needs a yearly mulch do it in late winter before seedlings appear. It is often difficult to identify many tiny plants before they get their first true leaves, so if there is a problem determining the difference between a seedling and a weed, wait until the plant is large enough to identify.

The garden should also be kept moist to allow germination, and this is not difficult if the garden has good soil containing plenty of organic matter. Seed can also be distributed throughout the garden. I often pick a handful of seed heads and distribute them around areas of the garden which the seeds can't reach by themselves. Large clumps of seedlings can always be lifted, thinned and replanted in other areas. Ideally, this should be done on a day when there is light rain.

Garden beds and paths in a natural garden should flow. There should be no hard lines and no formal definitions. Paths made of gravel, pressed dirt or stone will produce a natural impression. Gravel and stone allow more adventurous plants to seed beside or between the stones. Allowing a path to meander in a small garden creates the illusion that the garden is bigger than it actually is. Paths should also lead somewhere—to an ornament, garden seat or shady arbour.

Small gardens can also be made to look larger by a skilful use of plant texture.

Self-sown pathway plants have an informal quality

Small leaves create an illusion of space while larger leaves attract your attention, thereby reducing the sense of space in the garden. Do not rely completely on flower colour from annuals and perennials to create interest. Leaf texture, shape and differing hues of green add charm to a garden.

The central point of having a natural garden is the lack of obligatory maintenance associated with this gardening philosophy. The high maintenance precedent set by more formal gardens often inhibits rather than encourages those who have neither the time nor inclination to maintain their garden.

The range of freely self-seeding plants is immense. For areas of dappled shade you should include busy lizzie (*Impatiens wallerana*), honesty (*Lunaria annua*), *Viscaria* species, forget-me-nots, heartsease and *Helleborus* species.

Self-seeding plants for sunny areas include columbines (*Aquilegia vulgaris*), babies' tears (*Erigeron karvinskianus*), foxgloves (*Digitalis purpurea*), which tolerates sun or dappled shade, *Lychnis coronaria*, Queen Anne's lace (*Ammi majus*), red campion (*Silene dioica*), Iceland poppies (*Papaver nudicaule*), love-in-a-mist (*Nigella damascena*), Flanders poppy (*Papaver rhoeas*), Californian poppy (*Eschscholzia californica*), *Primula malacoides*, cosmos, species geraniums, Chinese forget-me-nots, evening primroses, mullein and cornflowers.

Clumps of perennials are essential for a natural garden and they multiply each year. Choose colours that complement your self-seeding annuals and use them with shrubs as structural plants in garden beds.

Chance collections of flowers spill onto the pathway

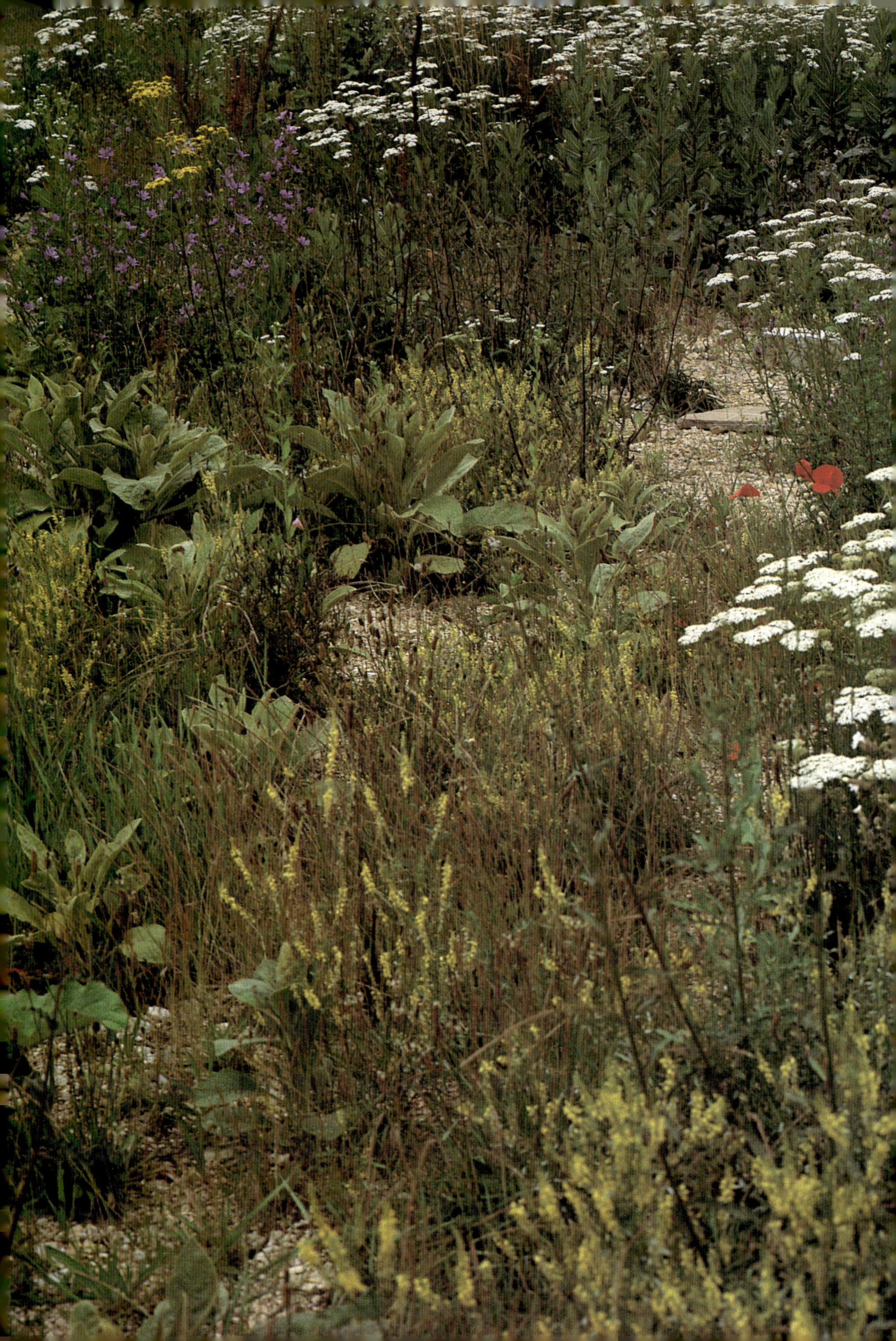

The Magic of Meadows

Lawnmowing is a boring and repetitive garden chore. Only a masochist could enjoy walking for hours behind a lawnmower as it spews fumes into the atmosphere. And the resulting clipped, overly neat lawn area is usually as boring as the task of mowing it. To escape the drudgery, simply close your eyes and imagine a field of wild and beautiful cornflowers, corn cockles or Flanders poppies in place of your lawn.

If you like the idea, you will have joined the growing numbers of people discovering the sheer pleasure of having a wildflower meadow. The only mowing required will be a path through the wildflowers as they are growing and a light mow over the meadow in early autumn when it has finished flowering and set seed.

The concept of a wildflower meadow is not new. Many early English naturalists created meadows in the wilder parts of their grounds. One of the oldest English meadows lies on the upper Thames River at Cricklade in Wiltshire, where it is part of a National Nature Reserve. Documentary evidence has revealed that this meadow has remained unploughed and untreated with chemicals for more than 800 years. It is thus the finest remaining example of a traditional lowland meadow in Britain. Seed is harvested directly from this meadow each year and sold in England as the Cricklade Mixture.

In America there is great enthusiasm for growing meadows, especially using native plants. Wildflowers are planted along the edges of roadsides and golfcourses instead of trees and shrubs. The seeds are literally sprayed onto banks in a liquid slurry form and left to naturalise.

The Botanical Gardens in Sydney has a meadow garden which is comprised of a combination of grasses and annuals. Included among the annuals are Iceland poppies, heartsease, forget-me-nots, larkspurs, primulas,

A combination of grasses, annuals and perennials forms a pretty meadow

godetias, English stocks, violas, calendulas and English daisies.

Correct preparation is essential before planting a meadow. The area should be free of weeds. Weeds can be removed with a hoe or spade, or you could spray the area with a weed killer like Zero. This preparation should be done before spring planting.

Another, most effective, and more organic method of ridding an area of weeds is to use newspaper covered with soil or compost mix. Lay the newspaper on top of the weeds. Three or four layers of paper is enough. If the layer is any thicker it will take the paper too long to break down and prevent the roots of the seedlings from breaking through. The newspaper actually smothers the weeds, blocking the light and preventing the weeds from photosynthesising.

Place a good compost mix at least 10 cm thick on top of the newspaper and water it well. I have recently made new garden beds using this method and placed 10 cm of mushroom compost on top of newspaper. After several weeks I dug though this to plant some old-fashioned roses and the newspaper had broken down enough to allow the roots of smaller seedlings to break through.

I also use newspaper when establishing pathways. I lay it very thickly on top of the grass and then place gravel on top. This method is more ecologically sound than using weedkillers.

Meadow mixes may be sown in late autumn or early spring. Once planted they generally regerminate naturally in early April, and late August or early September, when the soil temperatures are about 12 degrees Centigrade.

The most important factor when sowing the seed is that the soil and seed make contact. To facilitate the application of very fine seed, mix it with dry builder's sand. If you sow the seed too densely it will produce spindly plants which do not have enough room to grow.

The area must be kept moist while the seeds are germinating. Moisture can be retained quite easily if the seeds have been sown into a good compost mix or soil containing plenty of organic matter.

Seeds for a meadow may be bought individually or obtained in specially prepared mixtures from seed companies. There are some interesting combinations. These include the Wildflower Meadow Mix, which contains red Flanders poppies, orange Californian poppies, blue cornflowers, white Queen Anne's lace and blue alfalfa.

Aromatic Wildflower Meadow Mix contains the wonderful smells of dill, coriander and chamomile. The mixture also contains pink Shirley poppies and you could add borage for a touch of blue.

You do not need full sun to have a meadow. A shade-loving mix could include spring to summer flowering forget-me-nots, granny's bonnets, foxgloves, and heartsease.

The Wildflower Carpet Mix reaches a height of only 40 cm. Sown in October, it is capable of flowering from December to April and includes white alyssum, red paint brush, blue love-in-a-mist and Chinese forget-me-not.

Queen Anne's lace and cornflower is a most elegant combination. You could use blue cornflowers or a mixture which includes pink and white.

Some gardeners prefer the look obtained by using just one type of plant *en masse*. There are many annuals which will readily self-seed to produce a carpet of colour. Or you may choose different individual plants and make your own mixes.

Californian poppy (*Eschscholzia californica*) is certainly one of the easiest wildflowers to establish. The rich, orange flowers offset grey fern-like foliage. There are also varieties having cream or pink flowers.

Corn cockle (*Agrostemma githago*), reaches a height of 80 cm, will flower in 12 weeks from direct sowing and continues to flower for nearly 2 months. Cornflower, love-in-a-mist, Flanders poppy, plains coreopsis, Queen Anne's lace, cosmos, Shirley poppy and toadflax can be used to make beautiful meadows when planted by themselves or when mixed in different combinations.

If you like the appearance of daisies in your meadow you should include shasta daisies (*Chrysanthemum superbum*); feverfew (*C. parthenium*), which is a pretty, white daisy and red pyrethrum (*C. coccineum*), which has cerise pink flowers.

Ornamental grasses planted throughout the meadow add a nice touch. You could use blue fescue (*Festuca ovina* 'Glauca'), with its soft, blue-grey leaves; brown sedge grass (*Carex buchananii*); or fountain grass (*Pennisetum rueppli*), with its elegant, pink feathery flowers. *Carex* 'Frosty Curls' provides the lightest of green accents. The spiky foliage forms a bold clump, which reaches a height of 60 cm.

Do not stop at using these wonderful flowers for making meadows. They may be planted in garden beds for low maintenance gardening. I have seen them used in a wide garden bed adjoining a house and the beautiful display lasts from spring until summer. And the wonderful thing is, the choice of plant material is yours.

A meadow of Flander's poppies

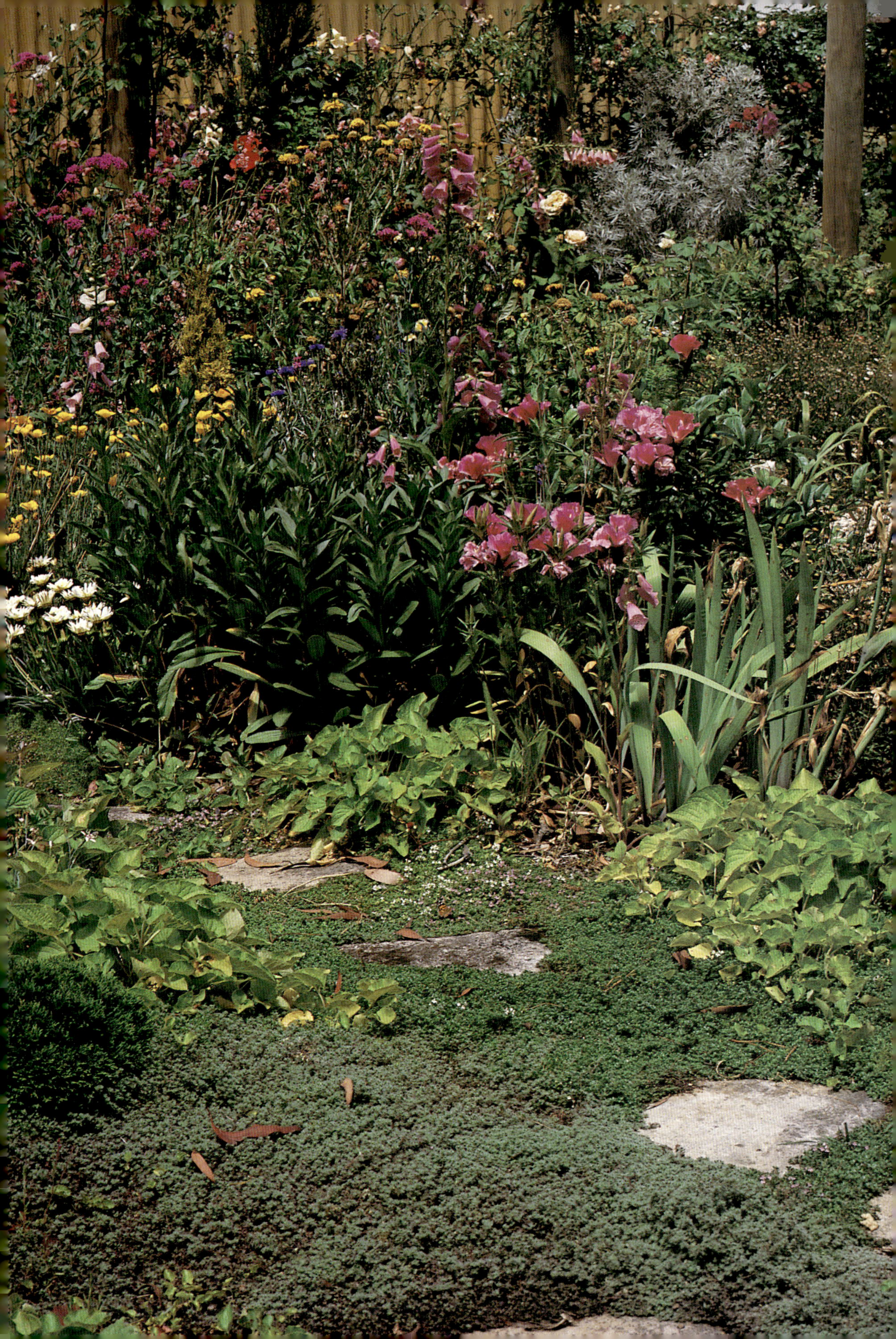

Fragrance in the Garden

PERFUME is an important aspect of creating garden enchantment and is one the garden's most subtle delights. There is certainly nothing nicer than walking through a garden and smelling the lingering perfumes of fragrant plants. Fragrant plants can become an obsession, as once you start placing them strategically throughout the garden you can always find one more spot where the reward of a new fragrance can be reaped.

Perfume in the garden adds another dimension and careful thought should be given to the placement of scented plants so that all the benefits can be received. Place them near doorways, windows, garden seats, in a courtyard or line the side of a pathway so that brushing against them will cause the air to be filled with scent.

Scented annuals and perennials will fill the spaces between perfumed trees, shrubs, climbers and old-fashioned roses. If they are carefully chosen, you can have fragrance throughout the year.

Often one scented plant is enough when placed near a window, as more than one fragrance can be over-powering and the delicacy of a particular perfume will be lost. Timing is also important; where possible choose plants which flower at different times so fragrances don't clash.

Of course, it does not always have to be flowers that give off the perfume. When weeding the garden there is nothing more enjoyable than brushing against the perfumed leaves of plants like scented-leafed pelargoniums, rosemary, lavender, and other herbs.

The heyday of the scented pelargoniums, or as they are more commonly called, scented-leafed geraniums, was the early nineteenth century, when they were included in every cottage, herb and scented garden. The wide range of leaf shapes, growth habits and perfumes make these indispensable additions to the

Different species of thyme are used to create a perfumed pathway

> *Hostas are valuable for shady areas and produce a beautiful perfume*

garden. Scented-leafed geraniums are often grown in gardens for the blind or other disabled persons where they add a fragrance that is both tantalising and appealing. If scented geraniums become too big, do not hesitate to prune them and they will form a bushier habit. The majority of the species will tolerate a little shade. They grow so easily from cuttings that I simply poke a cutting into the ground where I want it to grow.

There is a wide variety of scented-leafed geraniums available in cottage garden nurseries. Some of the more popular include the nutmeg-scented geranium (*Pelargonium fragrans*), which has small, slightly lobed, round, grey-green leaves and tiny white flowers; *P. x nervosum*, which has a strong scent of lime, small deep green leaves and lavender flowers; *P. odoratissimum*, loved for its strong apple scent, light green, ruffled leaves and tiny white flowers; *P. crispum*, which has small, curled and fluted leaves and small, pale lavender flowers and *P. tomentosum*, with its strong peppermint scent, large, grey-green, soft, velvety leaves and tiny white flowers.

Fragrant groundcovers can be substituted for grass lawns in small gardens, rewarding you with a delightful smell every time you walk on them. They can also be interspersed among the stones, bricks and gravel of pathways and courtyards.

Thyme is ideal as a groundcover or when used in pathways. You can use more than one species of thyme by combining different leaf and flower colours to create a pretty effect. Mountain or alpine thyme (*Thymus pseudolanuginosus*) has minute, grey, woolly leaves and lilac-pink flowers during late spring and summer. It is one of the best matting plants for steps and paths. Creeping or wild thyme (*Thymus serpyllum*) forms an attractive moss-green carpet of tiny leaves and has rosy-lilac flowers in late spring and summer. There are many cultivars of this species. 'Albus' has white flowers, 'Coccineus' has crimson flowers, 'Magic Carpet' has lilac-pink flowers and 'Aureus' is loved for its golden foliage. *T. citriodorus* 'Aureus' has, as its species name suggests, lemon-scented variegated foliage and mauve flowers.

Scented Annuals and Perennials

Antirrhinum majus (snapdragon)	Pretty, old-fashioned annual with a soft fragrance.
Cheiranthus cheiri (wallflower)	A sweetly perfumed annual with brightly coloured flowers.
Chrysanthemum coccineum (red pyrethrum)	The foliage has a strong perfume.
Dianthus barbatus (sweet William)	The carnation-like flowers appear from spring to summer.
Dianthus caryophyllus (carnation)	Carnations are loved for their rich perfume.
Dianthus chinensis (Indian pink)	The pretty flowers exude a sweet fragrance.
Dianthus deltoides (pinks)	Enchanting border plants. They look wonderful when placed beside a path.
Hedychium flavum (ginger lily)	The yellow flowers produce a spicy fragrance.
Hemerocallis species (day lily)	The lily-like flowers have a most delicate fragrance.
Hosta species	The flowers of hosta are sweetly-scented.
Lathyrus odoratus (sweet pea)	Among the most delicately scented of all the annuals.
Lobularia maritima (sweet alyssum)	White, purple or rose flowers virtually cover the plant throughout the year.
Malcomia maritima (Virginia stock)	A dainty annual with a soft fragrance.
Mathiola incana (stock)	A spring-flowering annual popular for its strong fragrance.
Nicotiana alata (flowering tobacco)	Grown for its heady evening scent.
Pelargonium species (scented-leafed geraniums)	The leaves of many species produce a strong perfume, especially when touched.
Reseda odorata (mignonette)	The orange-yellow flowers have a spicy aroma.
Thymus species	Strong-scented groundcovers.
Viola odorata (sweet violet)	The richly perfumed flowers appear in late winter.
Viola x wittrockiana (pansies)	The pretty, open-faced flowers have a sweet scent.

64 GARDEN ENCHANTMENT

Perfumed plants are ideal for use beside a pathway

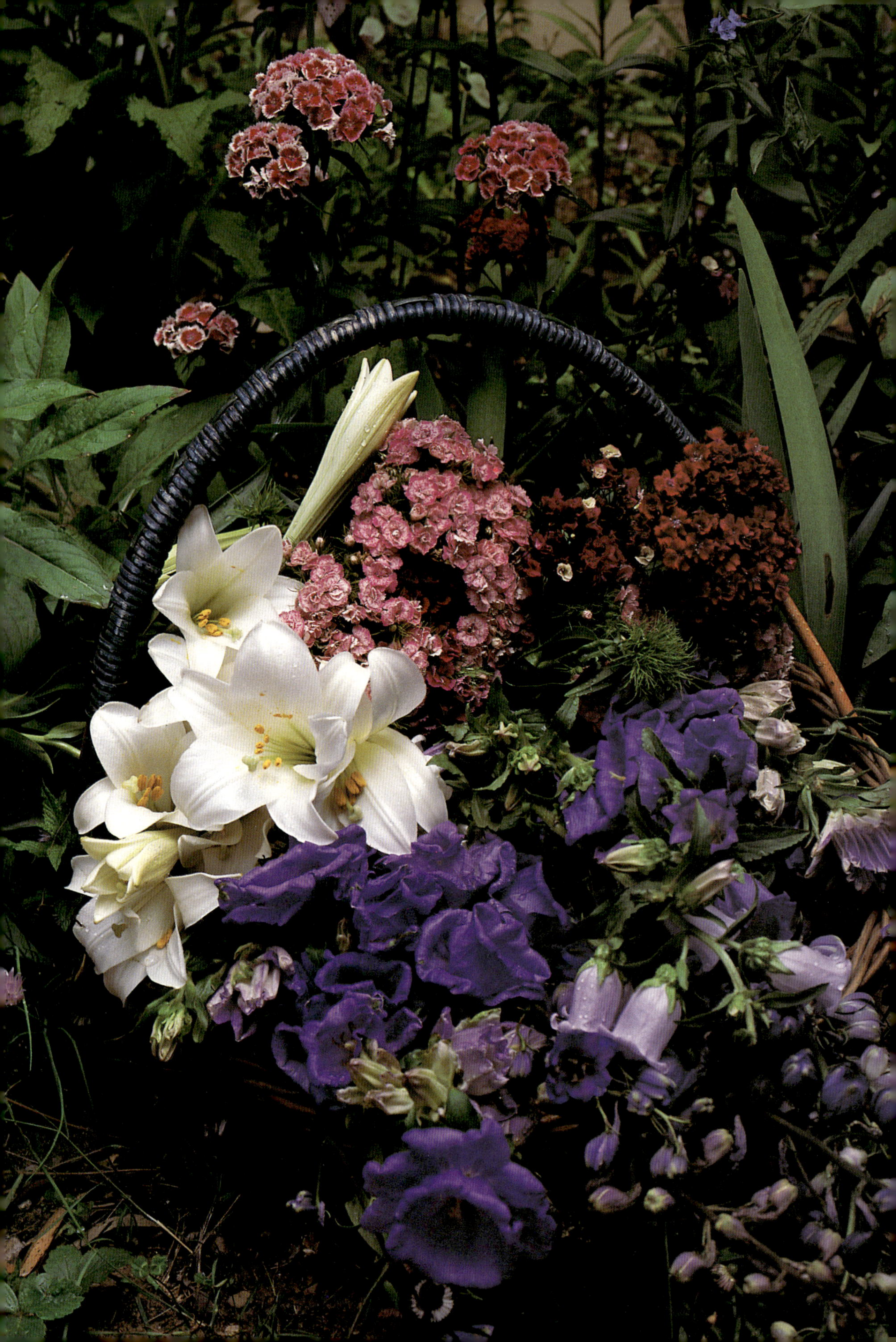

The Flower Arranger's Garden

FLOWER arrangement is an art that signifies a civilisation's development. It is an indication in all cultures that society has progressed to a high level of aesthetic sophistication and moved away from the cultivation of plants merely for food or other mundane purposes. The flower decorations found in great civilisations, both ancient and modern, reflect their values and preoccupations. The rituals of nearly all societies—weddings, funerals and harvest celebrations—have been enhanced by the wonderful sight and fragrance of flowers. And one of the great advantages of annuals and perennials is their capacity to be used in flower arrangements.

The earliest records of flower cultivation date back to 8000 BC. The first agricultural efforts of early civilisation were of a functional nature: plants were grown exclusively for food or medicinal purposes.

Gardens as an art of flower and plant cultivation developed much later and such gardens used an abundance of annuals and perennials. Decorative gardens first appeared in 1500 BC in Ancient Egypt, where civilisation had developed beyond subsistence level. The leisure time available to royalty and privileged members of society gave them the opportunity to cultivate and admire beautiful plants.

There are records of splendid formal gardens on the walls of Egyptian tombs. These gardens were walled and divided by avenues of trees. Vines grew over tall arbours and there were vivid masses of poppies, irises and cornflowers. Roses grew in such abundance that, in a later era, Egypt became the ancient world's chief supplier of plants and flowers.

Rose petals were used to carpet the floors and tables of Roman banquets and were brought by the shipload from Egypt. Archaeological evidence shows that the Ancient Egyp-

The art of flower arrangement depends entirely on the imagination and creativity of the arranger

tians decorated with cut flowers in vases. Bowls of flowers were placed on banquet tables and precious gold and silver vases were filled with the blossoms and buds of lotuses. These were offered as tributes to the pharaohs, kings and queens and were carried in processions.

The love of flowers is a tradition associated with English history from as early as the Middle Ages. Monks tended vast gardens, while small homeowners had what they called kitchen gardens that contained simple flowers like marigolds, violets, roses, irises and primroses. They were not used for flower arranging but for cosmetics, medicines, flavouring and food. Cut flowers at that time were only used for making garlands and for church rituals.

The art of arranging flowers was first documented in the seventeenth century, when the Dutch in particular painted wonderful informal arrangements. These wonderful arrangements included flowers and foliage as well as fruit and vegetables. Around the turn of the century the Impressionists like Cezanne, Van Gogh, Bonnard, Vuillard and Monet used flowers as the subjects of their paintings. Their paintings accurately re-created the colour of the plants and also attempted to suggest the ambience created by the arrangements.

The art of flower arrangement today depends entirely on the imagination and creativity of the arranger. The Australian climate lends itself to the production of a vast array of plant material. Throughout the year we have an incredible choice of flowers and foliage (both native and exotic) capable of being picked and brought indoors. There is nothing more satisfying than picking a bunch of flowers from the garden for indoors.

In my view the most successful flower arrangements are those that have been designed to suit a specific setting. The size, shape and colour of a flower composition should fit into its surroundings and be displayed in a container complementing both flowers and decor. A dainty arrangement on a small table is appealing and gains attention. A tall vase requires height in the arrangement, and a shallow bowl will display a short flower arrangement to its best advantage. Co-ordinating the colours of flowers with the colours of room furnishings increases the importance of both.

Foliage is most important in a flower arrangement as it brings flower colour to life. You can choose from the many shades of green or the softer, grey leaves of plants like lavender, santolina and artemisia. In autumn, branches of coloured leaves will bring a warm golden tone to the house. In my view a large vase of various types of foliage with different leaf types, colours and textures will often look more interesting than a vase of flowers. Such combinations are useful during winter in colder areas when flowers are scarce.

Pick flowers for indoors in the early morning or late afternoon, but not in the heat of the day. Flowers picked in the early evening last longer than ones picked in the morning because they have built up food reserves during the day. Cut the stems on a slant to provide a greater area for the absorption of water and so the stems will not sit squarely on the base of the container and make the taking in of water difficult. Flowers should be placed in water immediately after being picked.

Try to pick flowers when they are approaching perfection. Avoid buds that are too tight, as they might never open fully. On the other hand avoid flowers which are in full bloom, because their life expectancy after picking will be short. Flowers that bloom in clusters should be cut when half of the blooms are open.

Flowers with woody stems like antirrhinum, chrysanthemum, geranium, stock, wallflower and most flowering shrubs will be able to absorb water more easily if their stems are crushed and split for 7-8 cm at the base. Other flowers benefit if the stem is scraped and gently slit. These include anemone, aster, azalea, calendula, camellia, iris, larkspur, marigold and rose.

Flowers with hollow stems, or those which ooze sap when the stem is cut, last longer if the end of the stem is dipped in boiling water or seared in a flame. Such plants include Canterbury bells, dahlias, daisies, delphiniums, foxgloves, hydrangeas, Iceland poppies, lupins, phlox and zinnias. The hollow stems of lupin, foxglove and delphinium can be filled with water and sealed with a plug of cotton wool.

Tall flowers for bold arrangements include oyster plant (*Acanthus mollis*) whose purple and white flowers are produced on 60 cm spikes in early to mid-summer; hollyhock (*Alcea rosea*) which is available in single and double flowers in a wide range of colours; Canterbury bells (*Campanula medium*) which are available in shades of blue, pink, violet and white and flower from mid-spring to mid-summer; *Delphinium* species, the flowers of which are produced on 120-180 cm high stems in colours of white, pink, purple and blue; foxglove (*Digitalis purpurea*) whose pink, white, cream or purple flowers appear on spikes 90 cm tall; and viper's bugloss (*Echium fastuosum*), loved for its spikes of lilac-purple flowers with purple anthers.

The tall flower heads of red hot pokers (*Kniphofia* species) start appearing in summer and the interesting red and yellow flower heads look stunning in a tall vase. Numerous named and unnamed seedling forms are available, varying in height and colour. Most are variations of red and yellow.

A bunch of daisies always looks interesting in a vase. The marguerite daisy is available in white, pink or lemon. The flowers of *Aster novi-belgii* are also very attractive and will last as long as those of marguerite daisies.

It is hard to decide whether to pick the flowers or pick the seed pods of honesty (*Lunaria annua*) and love-in-a-mist (*Nigella damascena*). The violet-pink flowers of honesty are followed by seed pods the walls of which fall away when ripe to reveal a central, silvery membrane which glows with a pearly lustre. These pods will last indefinitely indoors. The flowers of love-in-a-mist may be white, light blue, rose-pink, mauve or purple. Both the flowers and the globe-shaped dried seed pods keep well when cut.

The fragrance produced by bunches of scented herbs like lavender, rosemary, marjoram, thyme and oregano will always be welcome in bathrooms or bedrooms. A large bunch comprised of scented geraniums, borage flowers and old-fashioned roses looks and smells wonderful. Bronze or green fennel will add leaf contrast to the arrangement. You can produce an interesting display by placing fennel flowers and foliage in a tall jar.

Pick flowers in the early morning or evening

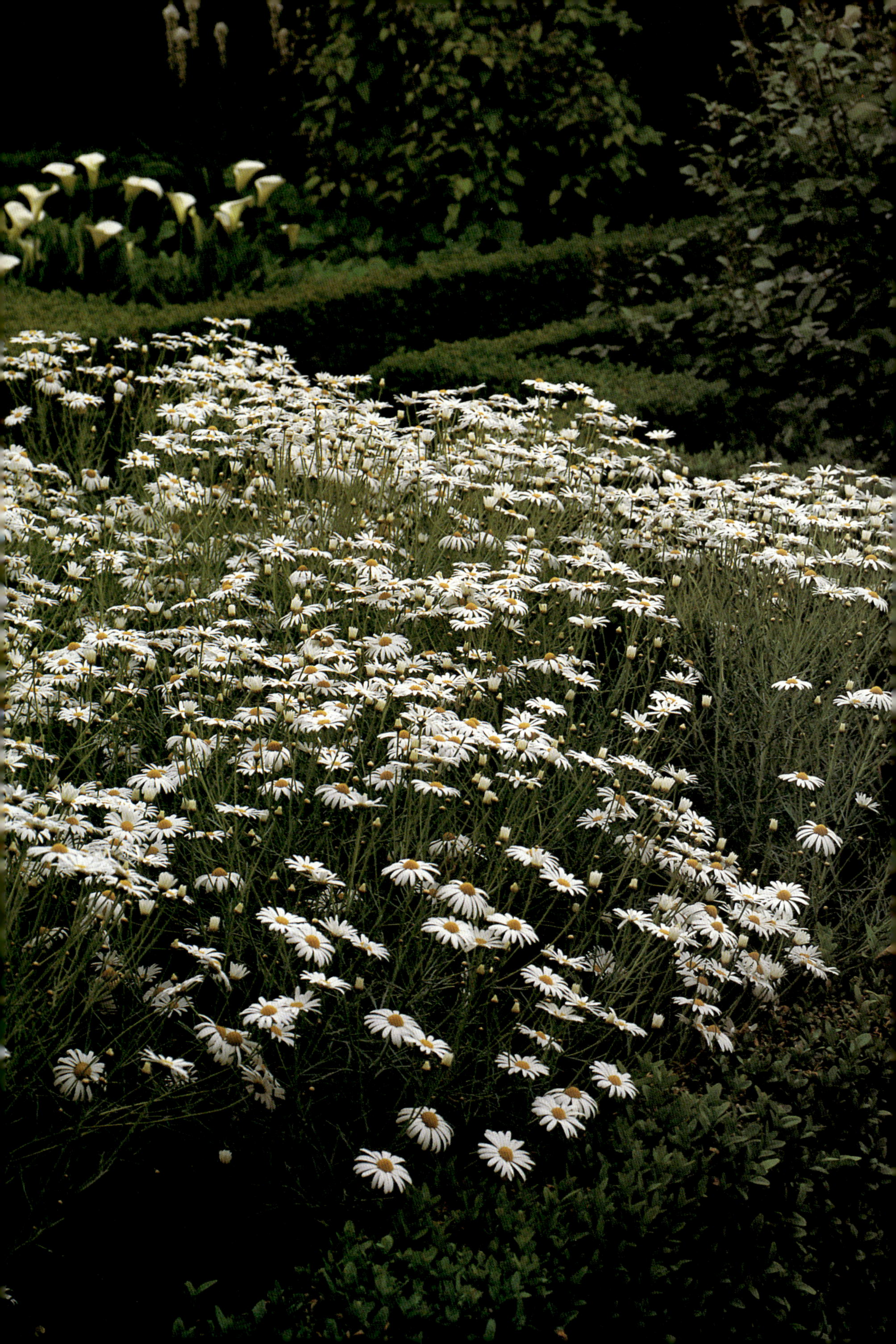

The Prolific Daisy

DAISIES are enchanting plants which have become even more popular in recent years with the increased interest in cottage and natural gardens. They lend themselves to many informal uses because they are often self-seeding and are suitable for use in plant combinations. I enjoy seeing daisies used freely and widely. Their proliferation throughout the garden seems natural given that they are such common plants which have outstanding connotations.

Daisies have traditionally been associated with purity, innocence and loyal love. Chaucer in his *Legende of Goode Women* has Queen Alceste transformed into a daisy because her virtues were as numerous as the daisy's petals.

According to German folk belief, daisies picked between 12 noon and 1 p.m. have magical qualities. They should be dried and carried as a good luck charm that will bring a successful result in any new undertaking.

In Christian legend the daisy sprung from Mary's tears during the flight into Egypt. In Christian medieval art, the flower was used as a symbol of the innocence of the Christ child.

Plants with daisy flowers were once classified as belonging to the Compositae family, but the name of the family has now been changed to Asteraceae. The older name alludes to the fact that each 'flower' is actually a composite structure consisting of a tight head of many tiny flowers known as florets. The 'petals' around the outside of the flower head are more correctly called ray florets, while the densely packed central florets are called disc florets.

The genus *Chrysanthemum* has many different species of delightful daisies. Included among these is *C. carinatum* (syn. *C. tricolor*), which has fine foliage and single or double flowers in

A mass planting of daisies creates an eyecatching effect

white and shades of yellow, mauve and red, with concentric rings in the centre near the disc in shades of red, yellow or purple. *C. carinatum* is easily raised from seed and reaches a height of 30-50 cm. Like most daisies it looks pleasing when planted *en masse* or can be used in clumps in a sunny border.

The red pyrethrum daisy (*C. coccineum* syn *C. roseum*) is a perennial with red, white or pink flowers. The thin, dark green foliage has a rather strong smell. Pyrethrum daisies are ideal for cutting and make stunning bedding plants. Old clumps can be divided in spring when new growth appears.

The marguerite daisy (*C. frutescens*) is one of the most popular daisies. It has always been an essential element in cottage gardens, where its simple flowers combine perfectly with all old-fashioned flowers, especially delphiniums, foxgloves, roses or cornflowers. This fast growing, shrubby perennial produces masses of flowers during spring, summer and into autumn.

The ray florets of the marguerite daisy are classically white around a central yellow disc, but there are many cultivars in shades of cream, yellow, pink and rosy carmine. Many of these have an enlarged, cushion-like central disc, often the same colour as the ray florets. These woody-based perennials last for a few years only, but are easily replaced by cuttings.

Cuttings can be taken any time of the year and placed in a sand and peat mixture. Because they take root so readily, I simply place my cuttings in the ground where I want them to grow and usually have a 90 per cent success rate.

Tip-pruning while the plant is young will encourage a bushier habit. To encourage new growth, cut the bush back by half its annual growth in early autumn when the flowers are diminishing.

Shasta daisies (*C. superbum* syn. *C. maxima*) are especially hardy. Natives of the Pyrenees, they have a very free-flowering habit and make an excellent cut flower. I find they make an ideal wildflower meadow because they are so hardy and have such a good spreading habit. The large clumps can be divided in late winter and early spring. The flowers of shasta daisies are comprised of 30-40 white ray florets with a golden central disc.

The variety 'Chiffon' has a double row of ray florets that are frilled and divided at the end, giving the flower a lacy appearance. A fully double variety called 'Ester Read' has the yellow disc replaced by a mass of fine, lacy, white florets which are heaped like a pincushion.

'Snowstorm' has the largest flowers, reaching 10 cm across. This is an improved form of the species, having broader, pure white ray florets and a golden disc.

Leopard's bane (*Doronicum plantagineum*) is invaluable for areas of light and filtered shade. It produces its yellow, 6 cm wide spring flowers above attractive, green, heart-shaped foliage. This fast-growing herbaceous perennial likes an acid, well-drained soil and should be cut back to near ground level during winter. It may be divided every few years.

I could not imagine a garden without babies' tears (*Erigeron karvinskianus*). This dainty little daisy is the perfect plant for the natural gardener. It self-seeds readily and the tiny plants will appear even in such unlikely places as the cracks in stone walls and between pathways. But no matter where it appears it always has a welcoming look.

Babies' tears make wonderful border plants or ground covers and will tumble happily over the sides of terracotta pots. The tiny pink and white daisies appear in spring and last until autumn. Babies' tears thrive in a sunny position. I have some in my garden growing in semi-shade which still flower, but not prolifically.

Blue flowers have an enchanting quality. Three pretty daisies which have flowers in shades of blue are Swan River daisy (*Brachycome iberidifolia*), blue daisy (*Felicia amelloides*) and Stoke's aster (*Stokesia*

Marguerite daisies displayed to perfection in an old copper

laevis). Incorporate them in a blue garden theme or combine them with white or yellow daisies for an arresting effect.

Swan river daisy, a native of Western Australia, has a low-growing habit which makes it an ideal groundcover. Plant it beside steps or pathways and allow it to tumble over the edges. The blue flowers are approximately 2 cm across, and other varieties have flowers in shades of pink or white. Cut Swan River daisy back after flowering and it will repeat its performance the following year.

Blue daisy is a small, bushy shrub reaching a height of approximately 75 cm. A native of South Africa, it will grow throughout Australia except in the coldest areas. The bright blue flowers (which are ideal for cutting) sit well above the foliage during summer, but you are also rewarded with flushes of flowers throughout the year. Trimming the bush occasionally between flowering flushes will keep it bushier.

The beautiful 10 cm wide summer flowers of Stoke's aster are a lavender blue and are borne on 60 cm long stems, which makes them ideal for cutting. The variety 'Alba' has white flowers, while 'Lilacina' has lilac-blue and 'Rosea' has pink.

For the sunny, dry garden, Cupid's dart (*Catananche caerulea*) is a must. The colourful display of blue, daisy-like flowers appears in summer and autumn.

Chamomile deserves a place in any garden for its prolific flowers and soft foliage. Mountain chamomile (*Anthemis montana*) has delicate, fern-like foliage and white daisy flowers with yellow centres. Flowering chamomile (*A. nobilis*) is a groundcover with aromatic, fern-like foliage. The white flowers have yellow centres and when dried they make a calming tea. The variety 'Treneague' does not flower and is often used as a lawn substitute. The fragrant, feathery foliage reaches a height of 6 cm and exudes a beautiful scent when trodden upon.

And last, but certainly not least, there are the sunflowers. They are indispensable when you need a bold display of yellow. Driving through Italy one becomes overwhelmed by the numerous fields of these flowers, all with their flower heads turning to face the sun. They are easily grown *in situ* from seeds and there are many varieties, some with double flowers.

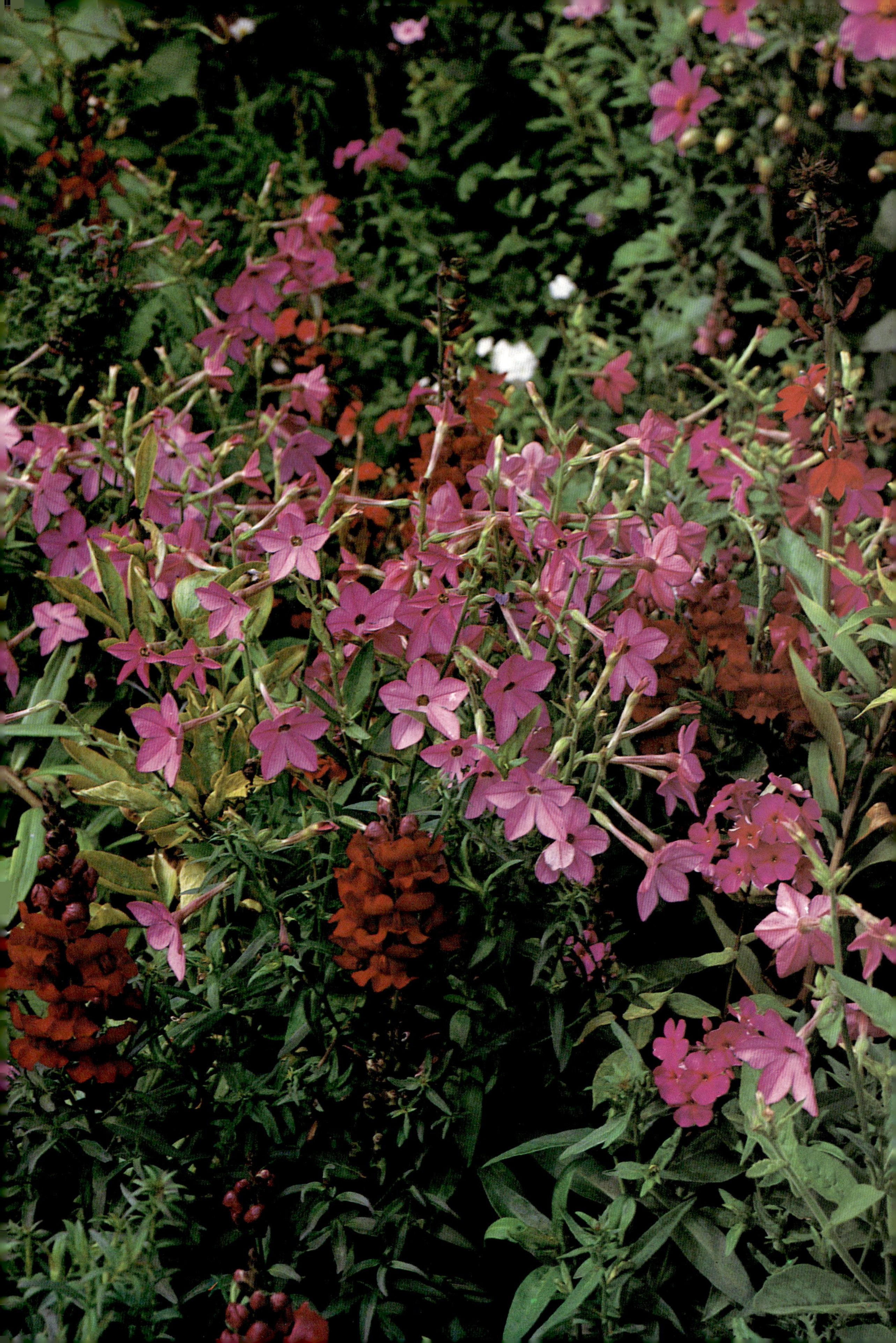

The Garden at Night

Spring and summer are wonderfully sensuous seasons in the garden. The colours, scents and sounds enhance our relaxation and enjoyment. These are the seasons where we can sit in the garden during the evening and become aware of the pleasing colour variations produced by the fading evening light.

When night falls, annuals and perennials with white or light coloured flowers will shine in the garden. And if these plants are positioned near a courtyard or window we can fully appreciate their almost magical qualities.

The perfume of many plants is stronger during the evening than it is during the day. For example, evening-scented stock (*Mathiola bicornis*) is not an inspiring looking plant during the day but it comes into its own at night, when its perfume is overpowering. Plant it near a window and the aroma will drift into the house. If sown in spring (except in tropical areas) it will be in full flower during mid-summer.

Night-scented tobacco (*Nicotiana alata*) is one of the hardiest of the tobaccos. The penetrating fragrance of this evocative flower will permeate the garden. Night-scented tobacco is a branching perennial which is usually grown as an annual. It carries panicles of tubular white flowers at the ends of long stems in spring and summer. The mid-green leaves are fairly large. For best results grow in full sun or half shade.

Nicotiana sylvestris is an annual which bears clusters of tubular, creamy-white flowers which are extremely fragrant at night.

The four-o'clock plant (*Mirabilis jalapa*) opens its flowers at just that time. They remain open at night and fade the following morning. The four o'clock plant thrives in hot areas and the highly perfumed crimson, pink, white or yellow flowers cover the mid-green foliage in summer.

In early times Londoners used to plant com-

The perfume of flowering tobacco is stronger at night

Babie's tears and shasta daisies glow softly in the evening light

mon mignonette (*Reseda odorata*) in window planters to quell unpleasant street odours. The perfume of the heavily musk-scented, yellowish brown flowers will pervade a patio, especially on a warm, humid night. Mignonette is particularly suited to pot culture and can even be brought indoors when in full flower.

The flowers of the evening primrose (*Oenothera* species), open in the late afternoon, as the common name suggests, and flower all night. *O. acaulis* has cup-shaped flowers which open white and gradually turn pink. This tuft-forming perennial reaches a height of only 20 cm. Although *O. speciosa* is commonly called the white evening primrose, its saucer-shaped flowers age to pink. It bears its flowers during summer and reaches a height of 45 cm.

The large flowers of *O. biennis* are like giant buttercups which shine through the night. A fast-growing biennial, *O. biennis* will often flower in its first year. It can self-seed very profusely but if it is culled in early spring when the new plants emerge it can be kept under control.

Moonflower (*Calonyction aculeatum*) is a beautiful, scented perennial climbing plant whose huge 15 cm, pure, white flowers unfold at dusk with a delicious fragrance that fills the air. This perennial climber reaches a height of 6 m and requires a warm, sunny position. Keep its roots cool with a mulch.

I have lined the sides of my front pathway with babies' tears (*Erigeron karvinskianus*), which is certainly a delightful perennial. This has not been an arduous task because of this plant's self-seeding habit. The multitudes of tiny white and pink flowers are very obvious at night. Babies' tears starts flowering in early spring and continues through summer. Cut large clumps of it back during winter to encourage more flowers and a bushier habit. And don't worry about its self-seeding habit causing over proliferation as small plants are very easy to remove. You may even be surprised at some of the interesting places in your garden in which babies' tears will spontaneously appear.

White-flowering perennials and annuals create a soft glow in the evening light. You might consider Japanese windflower (*Anemone x hybrida*), columbines, Michaelmas daisies, Marguerite daisies, shasta daisies, *Gypsophila paniculata*, perennial phlox, Stoke's aster or verbena.

Large silver-leafed plants create beacons in the darkening shadows. Plant wormwood (*Artemisia absinthium*) at the end of a path. The dominant splash of silver foliage will act like an evening lantern.

The flowers of evening primrose (Oenothera biennis) open at dusk and shine throughout the night

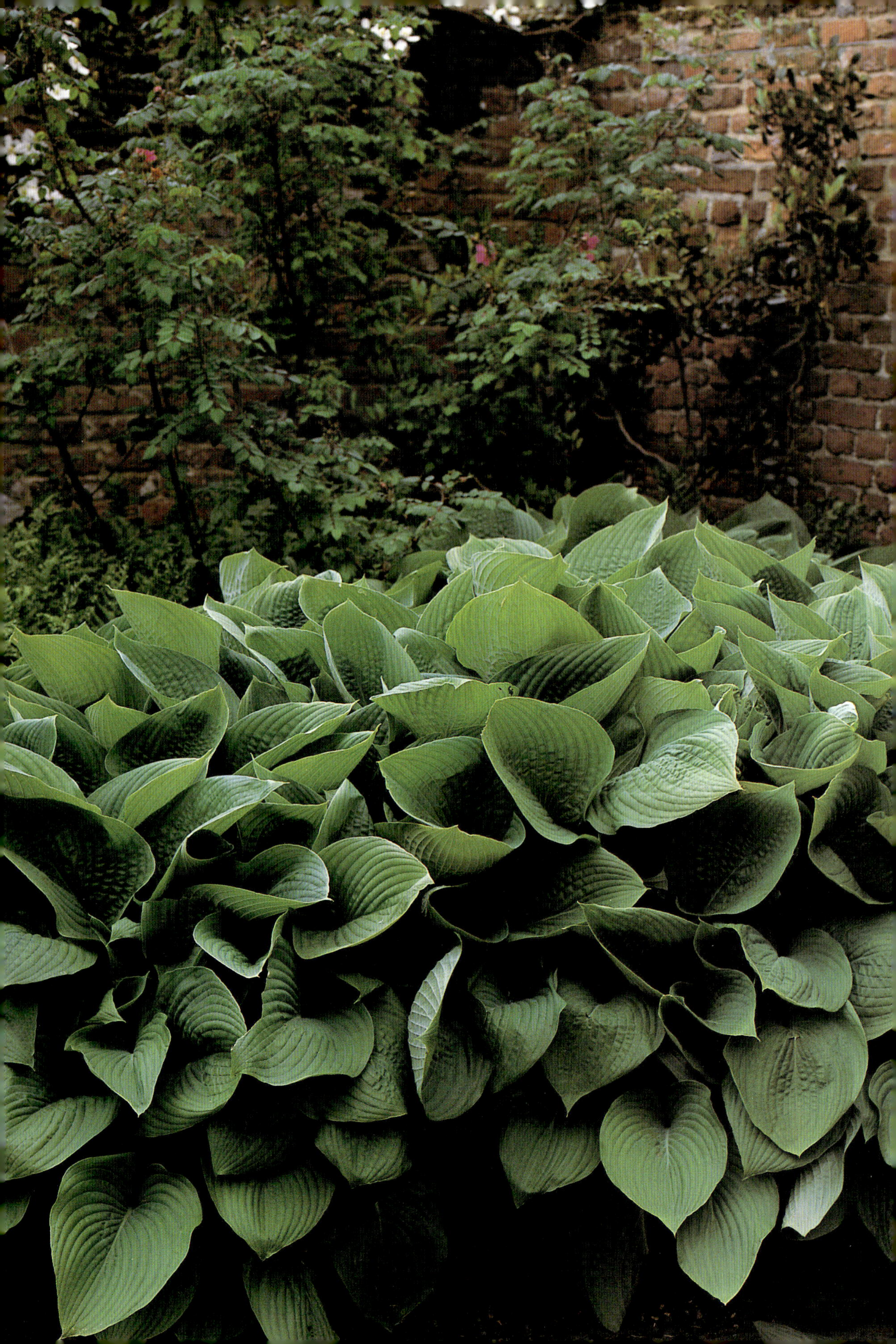

The Shade Garden

I₁ many gardens, shady areas represent a lost opportunity. Those who mistakenly believe that little will grow in the shade lose the chance to create pleasant and alluring areas full of unusual and beautiful plants.

Paradoxically, many shade-loving plants develop strength and beauty because of the light they have been denied. They have adapted themselves by developing large leaves to enhance the process of photosynthesis, and they have acquired a diverse range of foliage and flower types. The large, strong leaves make the plants visually attractive and their usually pale flower colouring lends itself to a subtle and mysterious sense of place.

Although shade is a general word for any darkening effect, the discriminating gardener should become aware of different types of shade. One should understand differences in the quality of light, the reasons for such differences and the effects they may have on the soil.

Shade cast from a building or wall is permanent and the most difficult to come to terms with, as it is dense and solid. Dense shade caused by tree foliage, on the other hand, is easy to change by altering or thinning the heads of the offending trees. Thus deep shade can become medium, light or dappled shade. Thinning a tree will not change the overall size of it but will reduce its thickness. Do this during winter, taking care not to spoil the tree's appearance. Select the bough you wish to remove, then stand back from the tree and imagine what it would look like with the bough removed.

There are also two varieties of shade which are determined by the location. Different microclimates can exist side by side in gardens. Damp shade, which generally receives no sun at all and always has moist soil, can co-exist next to dry shade, found under eaves and close to buildings.

Damp, densely shaded soil can become dark

Hostas and columbines thrive in the shade

and sour because the circulation of the air is restricted. Correct this before planting by turning the soil a couple of times. Allow a break in between turns to permit air circulation. Shaded soil can also become very acidic, but this is easy to check with a soil-testing kit.

If the soil is extremely wet, it is worthwhile spending the time to make permanent alterations with PVC drainage pipes.

Soil in shaded areas often lacks nutrients and needs supplements of fertilisers. Mulches of cow or chicken manure and compost are ideal, as they attract earthworms which in turn help to aerate the soil. As the mulches break down they also add structure to the soil, encouraging better drainage. This is most important in dry shaded areas, as organic matter will help to retain moisture.

Dappled shade under trees may be turned into woodland areas with the clever use of perennial groundcovers or annuals. You could have drifts of violets combined with Italian bellflower and plectranthus. Or plant groundcovers like ajuga or lamium.

Violets thrive in dappled shade under deciduous trees and will spread to form a close carpet. *Viola odorata* is the original violet from which many varieties have been formed. It has dark purple flowers and there is also a white form. Flower colours among the varieties include magenta, lilac, pink, blue and red-violet. You can use the native violet (*Viola hederacea*) which has pretty, white to pale mauve flowers with contrasting violet centres.

Intersperse bellflower (*Campanula poscharskyana*) through the violets. The leaves of Italian bellflower are very similar to those of the violets. Its star-shaped, sky blue flowers appear from spring through summer.

Allow *Plectranthus oertendahlii* to ramble through plants like the ones mentioned above. Plectranthus has large, dark green leaves with a purple underside. During autumn, lace-like spires of light mauve flowers sit above the leaves to create the daintiest impression. Plectranthus spreads by layering as its stems touch the ground. If it starts to take over the violets and bellflower it may be thinned easily. I have seen this plant thriving in a cool climate garden under large conifers where nothing else will grow. Propagation is as easy as removing a stalk and popping it in the ground.

Lamium galeobdolon is among the most rapidly spreading groundcovers. But place it where there is no possibility that it will choke other plants. It spreads quickly by means of long, arching stolons to form a dense cover. The evergreen leaves which are splashed with silver look attractive throughout the year and are complemented

Hostas make an interesting border in this shade garden

Helleborus species which have naturalised under trees

Shade-loving Annuals and Perennials

Name	Shade requirements	Name	Shade requirements
Acanthus mollis	semi	*Impatiens wallerana*	semi
Aconitum napellus	semi	*Lamium galeobdolon*	full or semi
Ajuga reptans	full, semi, dappled	*Liriope spicata*	dappled
Alstroemeria aurea	light	*Lobularia maritima*	dappled
Anemone blanda	full	*Lunaria annua*	full or semi
Anemone x hybrida	full, semi	*Lupinus* hybrids	light
Aquilegia vulgaris	semi	*Malcomia maritima*	semi
Astilbe x arendsii	full, semi	*Myosotis sylvatica*	full, semi or dappled
Bellis perennis	semi	*Nemophila menziesii*	semi
Bergenia schmidtii	full, semi	*Nicotiana alata*	light
Campanula isophylla	dappled, partial	*Nigella damascena*	semi
Campanula medium	light	*Ophiopogon japonicus*	semi or dappled
Centranthus ruber	light	*Phlox paniculata*	light
Consolida ambigua	light	*Physostegia virginiana*	semi
Convolvulus mauritanicus	dappled	*Plectranthus oertendahlii*	full or semi
Dicentra spectabilis	full	*Polygonatum multifolium*	full, semi
Digitalis purpurea	semi	*Primula malacoides*	semi
Doronicum plantagineum	partial	*Primula x polyantha*	semi, dappled
Filipendula purpurea	semi	*Saponaria officinalis*	light
Fragaria indica	dappled	*Saxifraga umbrosa*	semi or dappled
Hedera species	full, semi or dappled	*Torenia fournieri*	partial
		Tropaeolum majus	partial
Helleborus species	full, semi	*Verbena x hybrida*	partial
Hosta species	full, dappled	*Viola hederacea*	semi or dappled
Hypericum calycinum	full, semi or dappled	*Viola odorata*	dappled
		Viola x wittrockiana	dappled
Impatiens balsamina	semi		

by the beautiful, whorled spikes of soft yellow flowers in spring.

In all its forms, ajuga is a marvellous plant which, once established, forms dense cover. During spring its erect spikes carry tubular blue flowers. Ajuga will even grow in dense shade beneath evergreen trees or under eaves. The green foliage has a rosette formation and the plants spread by rooting at the stem joints. *Ajuga reptans* 'Alba' has glossy leaves that are offset beautifully when the spikes of white flowers appear. Several interesting cultivars are also available; 'Atropurpurea' is a purple-leafed form

and 'Multicolor' has bronze, pink and cream variegated foliage.

All the species of helleborus can be used to make a delightful woodland setting and their winter flowers last for months. The dainty, large, saucer-shaped, white, pink tinged flowers of *Helleborus niger* sit on top of a tall stem. *Helleborus orientalis* is a pretty plant, usually producing cream flowers splashed with purple. Helleborus multiply well from a short, creeping root stock. Their capacity to self-seed is a worthwhile bonus.

Bergenias (*Bergenia x schmidtii*) look

pretty in a woodland setting or can be placed close together as a groundcover in dry shade under eaves. The pink winter flowers stand on stalks above the large, mid-green leaves.

There is nothing prettier than drifts of primulas under trees. Primulas will thrive with only morning or afternoon sun. *Primula x kewensis* is the product of a cross made at Kew Gardens in 1898 between the Himalayan *Primula floribunda* and the Arabian *Primula verticillata*. Its fragrant yellow flowers droop from 30 cm stalks.

Polyanthus (*Primula x polyantha*) start flowering in early winter when other flowers are scarce. The colour range includes white, cream and shades of yellow, red, pink, orange and blue.

For cool climate gardens you can also grow the Chinese primrose (*P. sinensis*), English primrose (*P. vulgaris*) and the Japanese candelabra primrose (*P. japonica*).

For a grassy look in dappled shade you could use mondo grass or lily turf. Mondo grass (*Ophiopogon japonicus*) reaches a

Solomon's seal (Polygonatum) thrives in the shade

height of 15 cm and has dark green leaves and lilac flowers. It is more tolerant of shade than lily turf and can be grown in moist or dry soil. Set the plants 15 cm apart, and except for watering during dry times, they are practically maintenance-free. White mondo grass (*O. jaburan*) is taller-growing (30 cm) and has white summer flowers. There are forms with blue flowers, striped golden foliage and striped white foliage.

Lily turf (*Liriope spicata*) is an evergreen perennial which has 35 cm tall, fine leaves and bell-like lilac flowers from summer to autumn. The deep green leaves of blue lily turf (*Liriope muscari*) reach a height of 30 cm. Its mauve flower spikes appear at the same time as lily turf and have a similar appearance to grape hyacinths. Plant both species 20 cm apart.

London pride (*Saxifraga umbrosa*) is a very hardy old-fashioned plant which deserves to be more popular. It forms rosettes of rather thick, fleshy mid to dark green leaves and its 45 cm flower stems produce loose panicles of small, pink, starry flowers in spring and early summer. It will thrive in filtered shade under trees.

The woodland anemone (*Anemone blanda*) and the Japanese anemone (*Anemone x hybrida*) make wonderful drifts as do forget-me-nots and viscaria. The pretty purple or white flowers of honesty (*Lunaria annua*) are followed by attractive silver seed pods.

THE SHADE GARDEN 85

The light green flowers of helleborus are accentuated in the shade

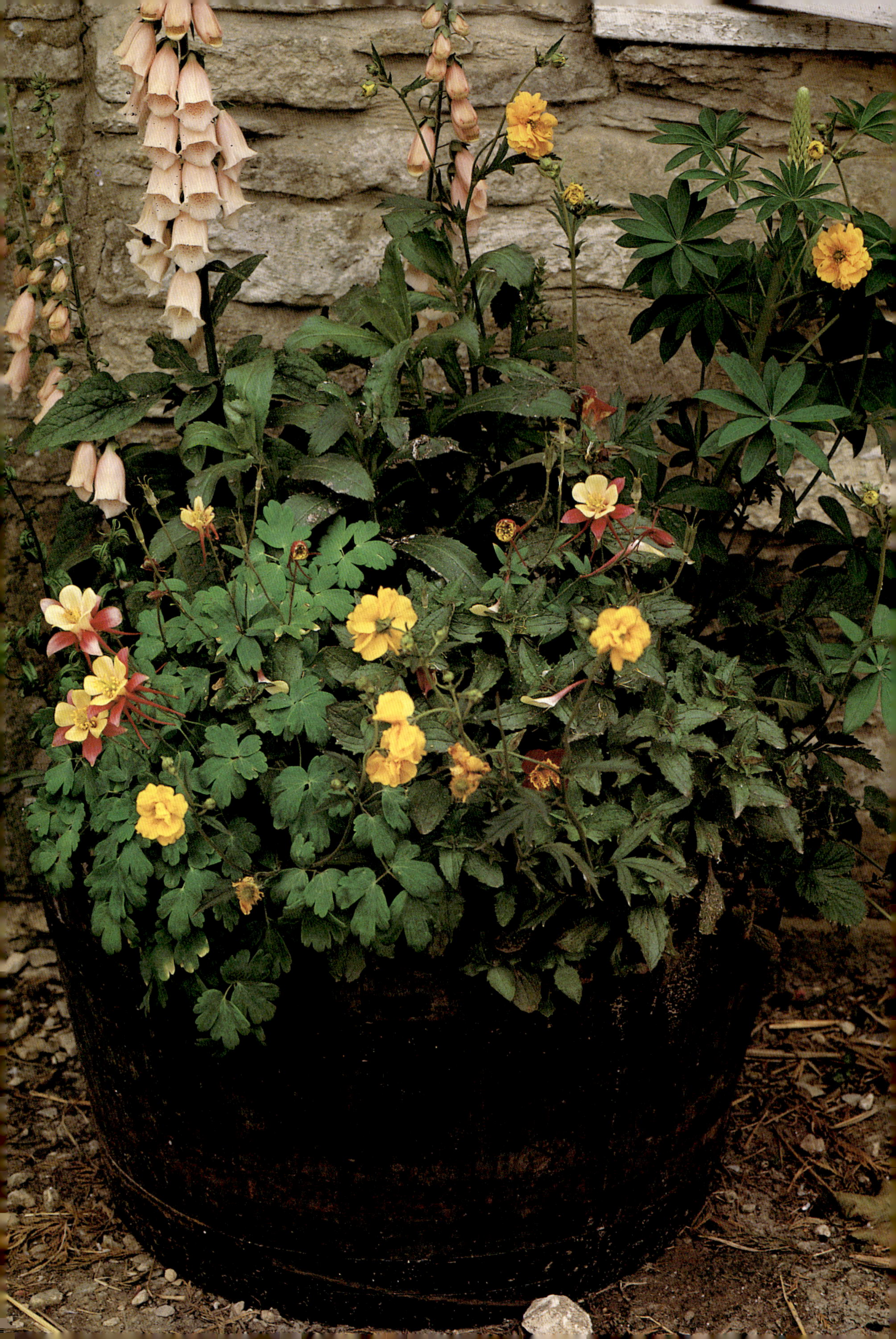

Potted Perfection

Annuals and perennials in pots are a constant source of delight. They bring life and colour to the garden throughout the year and can be moved to become features when in flower. There are many ways you can use pots in landscape design. They can be treated in a formal manner by arranging them in symmetrical groups or used informally in clusters. Let the choice and arrangement of containers reflect the mood of your garden.

Large pots dotted through the garden always create an element of surprise. And in many small, paved city gardens pot plants are essential to the very existence of the garden. Some container plantings are relatively permanent as the plants can stay in the same pot for many years. Other arrangements are planted purely for seasonal colour and may be replanted when the flowers have passed their peak. On the other hand, some containers are so handsome they can stand on their own as sculpture.

Stone and terracotta pots have a natural appearance and are among my favourites. The only problem with terracotta pots is their porous nature which necessitates constant watering of the plants contained in them. One method of avoiding this necessity is to line the inside of the pot with black plastic. But do not line the bottom of the pot as this will impede drainage.

Large pots can become dramatic features. One strategically placed pot containing an interesting standard plant like a marguerite daisy is often all that is needed.

The versatile nature of pots allows them to contain almost any type of plant. Use pots full of annuals to provide splashes of seasonal colour. Choose flower colours that complement your existing garden scheme, or if you are placing pots in a small courtyard, make sure flower colours complement the colour of your house and garden furniture.

Marigolds (*Tagetes* species) always look

A wooden tub brimming with perennials

> *A simple container is often more appealing than one that is laden with confusing detail*

stunning in pots and you do not have to grow the varieties with very bright and large flowers. There is a wide colour range which includes lemon, yellow and orange and the flower heads may be single or double. 'Snowdrift' is a pretty white marigold and 'Fragrance' has lemon-scented foliage and masses of dainty single flowers. The seed may be directly sown into the pot from spring to summer.

I always plant out a few containers of the pot or English marigolds (*Calendula officinalis*) because of their long flowering period and because the petals are delicious when tossed through salads or used in egg dishes. Bought in punnets in spring, they will flower in about five to six weeks. The colour range includes pastel shades of yellow, gold and orange. Cutting the flowers back to a node on the stem will encourage more flowers.

There is no need to have only one type of plant in a pot. A variety of different flowers is most eye-catching. Combine blue or white salvia with cosmos and allow lobelia to drape over the side of the pot. Cosmos is available in white or pink and will produce superb colour until autumn. Yellow and lemon marigolds always look good in association with dark blue petunias and blue lobelias.

Nasturtiums are easy to grow and will thrive in pots placed in full sun or semi-shade. The variety 'Fragrant Gleam' has a semi-trailing habit and is ideal for cascading in hanging baskets. The fragrant blooms are available in yellow or red and are also ideal for cutting. The marbled leaves of nasturtium 'Alaska' appeal whether or not its red flowers are in bloom.

Impatiens is ideal for shady corners but will do equally well in sun. The new varieties have a compact, tidy, base-branching habit and good flower size and quality. Once they start flowering they are rarely without a flower. 'Blush' is among the fastest-flowering and the largest of all the impatiens. 'Blue Pearl F1' exhibits a lovely pastel shade of blue. It makes a beautiful companion to 'Blush' or the white variety but looks striking by itself.

A large pot full of daisies can look most impressive. The marguerite daisy (*Chrysanthemum frutescens*) is available in shades of pink, white or lemon and for shades of blue you cannot surpass the Swan River Daisy (*Brachycome iberidifolia*), blue daisy (*Felicia amelloides*) and Stoke's aster (*Stokesia laevis*). Babies' tears (*Erigeron karvinskianus*), with its dainty, daisy-like flowers is invaluable for hot areas, as are pelargoniums. There is a large colour range and the scented geraniums are invaluable for their scented leaves and pretty flowers.

Group plants together that have contrasting foliage textures. Interesting groupings can be formed by contrasting form and habit. Upright and bushy plants should be planted near prostrate and cascading ones.

Low-growing, tufted or spreading annuals or perennials can be placed at the base of trees and shrubs planted in pots. Japanese mondo grass, violas, campanulas, lobelias or nasturiums are suitable for this purpose.

Success with potted plants is assured if you start with a good potting mixture. I usually add about $\frac{1}{3}$ cow manure to $\frac{2}{3}$ potting mixture. This supplies extra nutrients to the plant. Add Debco Water Storing Granules to the potting mix. These store water and release it to plants. Debco also make a hanging basket mix with the water storing granules already added and these granules significantly extend the time between waterings.

Apply a soluble plant food once a month when watering, except in the case of annuals, which appreciate a dose of half the recommended amount every two weeks.

Leaf colour and texture produce an interesting contrast with the timber of the container

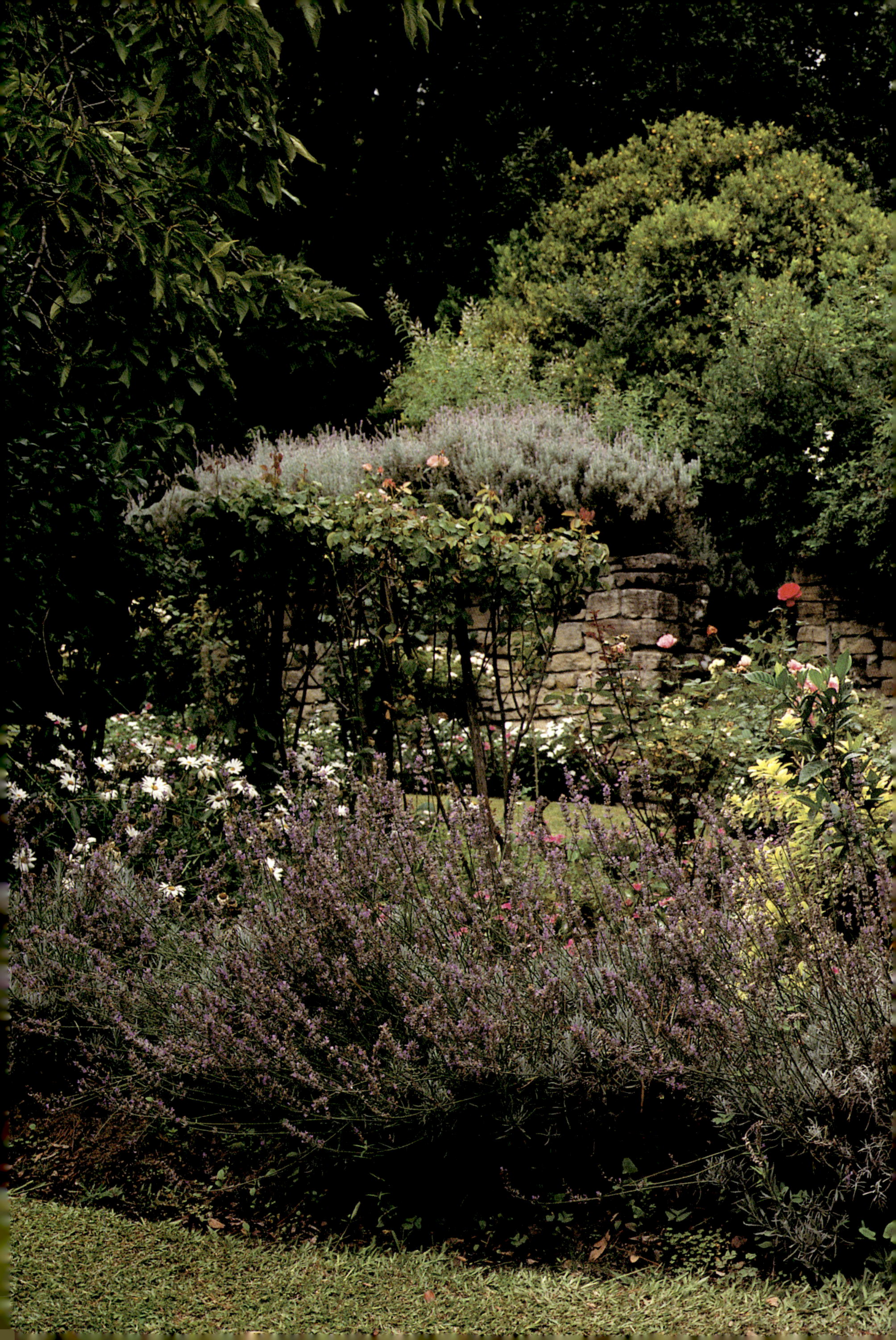

Herbs in the Garden

Herbs are among the most enchanting plants and to my mind are indispensable to any garden. Their fragrance and beauty add immediate appeal to garden plantings. Many herbs have a dainty appearance and leaf colours varying from grey to dark green. Foliage texture is also variable, as herbs like chervil and tansy have a very fine, fern-like foliage while sorrel or comfrey have larger, bolder leaves. When planted among other annuals and perennials they will create some beautiful foliage combinations.

The majority of herbs are annuals and perennials and do not need to be grown in a separate garden bed. Their flowers attract bees and butterflies to the garden and their fragrant leaves are a delight to brush against when working in the garden.

Herbs like thyme, pennyroyal and chamomile can be used as herbal lawns or for interplanting between stepping stones. One may also use them to make a fragrant footrest beneath the garden seat.

When it comes to the preparation of food, herbs have seemingly endless practical applications. Many herbs also have proven medicinal and restorative properties.

Given their many qualities, it is not surprising that a number of civilisations throughout history have imbued herbs with religious significance. Even in Britain the production of herbs was associated with monasteries, particularly after the sixth century. The domestication of herbs, however, can be traced to man's earliest horticultural activities.

The range of plants grown as herbs is much smaller than it was even several hundred years ago. There was then a harmonious relationship between botany and medicine that created the need for medicinal and culinary plants in every garden. As all gardens included such plants, there was no concept of a distinct herb garden.

A herb is usually defined as a special type of

Lavender makes an excellent garden border

Bees and butterflies are attracted to the herbs which have been interplanted throughout the garden

Companion Planting with Herbs

Anise	Sow coriander and anise seeds together to assist germination.
Basil	Do not plant near rue.
Borage	Plant in the strawberry patch.
Caraway	The long roots of caraway help to break down heavy soils. Do not plant next to fennel.
Chamomile	Compatible with onions and cabbage.
Chervil	Grow chervil with carrots.
Chives	Plant underneath apple trees and near roses.
Coriander	Sow anise and coriander together to assist germination.
Dill	Plant dill next to cabbage.
Fennel	Fennel has an adverse effect on tomatoes, bush beans, kohlrabi, caraway and wormwood.
Hyssop	A good insect repellent in the flower garden.
Marjoram	Marjoram has a beneficial effect on most vegetables and flowers.
Parsley	Plant near roses and tomatoes.
Rosemary	Grow near sage.
Rue	Do not grow rue near basil.
Sage	Grow near cabbages. Do not plant next to cucumbers.
Savory	Plant next to onions and green beans.
Tansy	Add to the compost heap to assist fermentation.
Thyme	Thyme is beneficial to most plants in the garden.
Yarrow	Yarrow increases the aromatic quality of most herbs.

plant used predominantly in cooking. But in fact any herbaceous or woody plant which is aromatic in any of its parts, or which is considered to have culinary, medicinal or cosmetic value, can be regarded as a herb.

In my view, there is nothing nicer than a traditional herb garden, but not many gardeners have the space. You may still achieve the effect by laying out the garden traditionally and not restricting it to herbs only. Grow your annuals and perennials among the herbs and you will be well rewarded.

Traditionally, separate herb gardens were paved and laid out in a formal chessboard pattern or as circular gardens arranged like the spokes of a wheel. The herbs grown in the squares of a chessboard pattern can vary in height without encroaching upon or overshadowing their neighbours. Each plot is generally about 1 m square but the amount of space needed will be determined by the overall size of your garden and your specific herb requirements.

Hedges of lavender, rosemary, sage or bay may be grown as a protective perimeter of the garden. A sundial, birdbath or seat may be used as the centrepiece of a formal garden. A seat allows you to appreciate the beautiful aromas and to watch the butterflies which are invariably attracted to herb flowers during the heat of the day.

Complicated designs may be used but it is advisable to draw a pattern before implementing any plan. Intricate designs like those used in the Elizabethan knot gardens can be fascinating. The Elizabethan garden beds were edged with dwarf boxwood, thyme, violets and santolina. Plants within the beds were arranged so that the maximum effect was derived from the juxtaposition of each kind of plant with its

The border for this pathway is comprised of a delightful mixture of herbs

neighbours. Contrasting leaf patterns add dimension and texture to the overall design.

Such strict formality is not necessary, and you may choose to cultivate your plants in herbaceous borders or garden beds.

Smaller herbs like gold leaf marjoram or thyme make excellent ground covers or edging plants. Angelica and artemisia can be used as background plants or simply to add interest and structure to the bed.

Angelica (*Angelica archangelica*) creates a dominant display in garden borders. Its large, light green leaflets are deeply dissected and divided. The ridged stems are hollow and rounded and umbrella-like heads of yellow-green flowers appear during summer. Angelica will thrive in semi- shade.

Artemisias were standard plants in early herb gardens. Mugwort (*Artemisia lactifolia*) is a useful plant for the back of a border. The deeply serrated leaves are green on top and downy underneath.

The silvery, hair-like leaves of southernwood (*Artemisia absinthium*) are indispensable for adding silver to a garden. Both artemisias are valued for their beautiful, aromatic foliage.

Bergamot (*Monarda didyma*) is a very attractive herbaceous plant with densely whorled heads of bright scarlet flowers. A perennial, it will readily spread to form a large clump. The fresh leaves added to a pot of tea impart a wonderful aroma.

No garden would be complete without sage, which is used widely in cooking. Sage (*Salvia officinalis*) is a woody perennial plant with oblong, woolly, grey-green leaves. It reaches a height of 90 cm or more and the purplish-blue flowers appear on tall spikes. In the seventeenth century an infusion made from the flowers was believed to make men immortal. The leaves of red sage (*S. officinalis* 'Purpurea') are tinged with violet-red. Although this is now usually grown for its decorative properties, in early times it was more valued in the kitchen than the green form. Clary sage (*S. sclavea*) looks good when planted next to catmint and a bunch picked and brought indoors brings a freshness to bathrooms and kitchens.

Plant lemon balm (*Melissa officinalis*) near a seat in a meditative part of the garden as it tends to create a tranquil effect. It is a charming and fragrant perennial with dark green leaves which have a distinctive lemon scent and creamy flowers during summer. It makes a good groundcover as it spreads easily but virtually dies down during winter.

Herbs are among the easiest plants to grow and have few specific cultivation needs. With little exception, herbs thrive in a free-draining soil and enjoy a sunny location. Taller species should be given protection from the wind.

The perfumed leaves of many herbs are most appealing

Herbs grown in containers look most attractive and are ideal for gardeners who have limited space. Container-grown herbs also give you the capacity to meet their cultivation needs throughout the year as the containers can be moved around to catch the sun. Always use a good, free-draining potting mixture and feed the plants every four weeks with a complete soluble plant food.

At the end of the season herbs can be dried easily by taking a bunch of one kind of herb, tying the ends of the stems together with string and hanging the bunch upside down in a warm place away from direct sunlight. The bunches of herbs look wonderful in the kitchen.

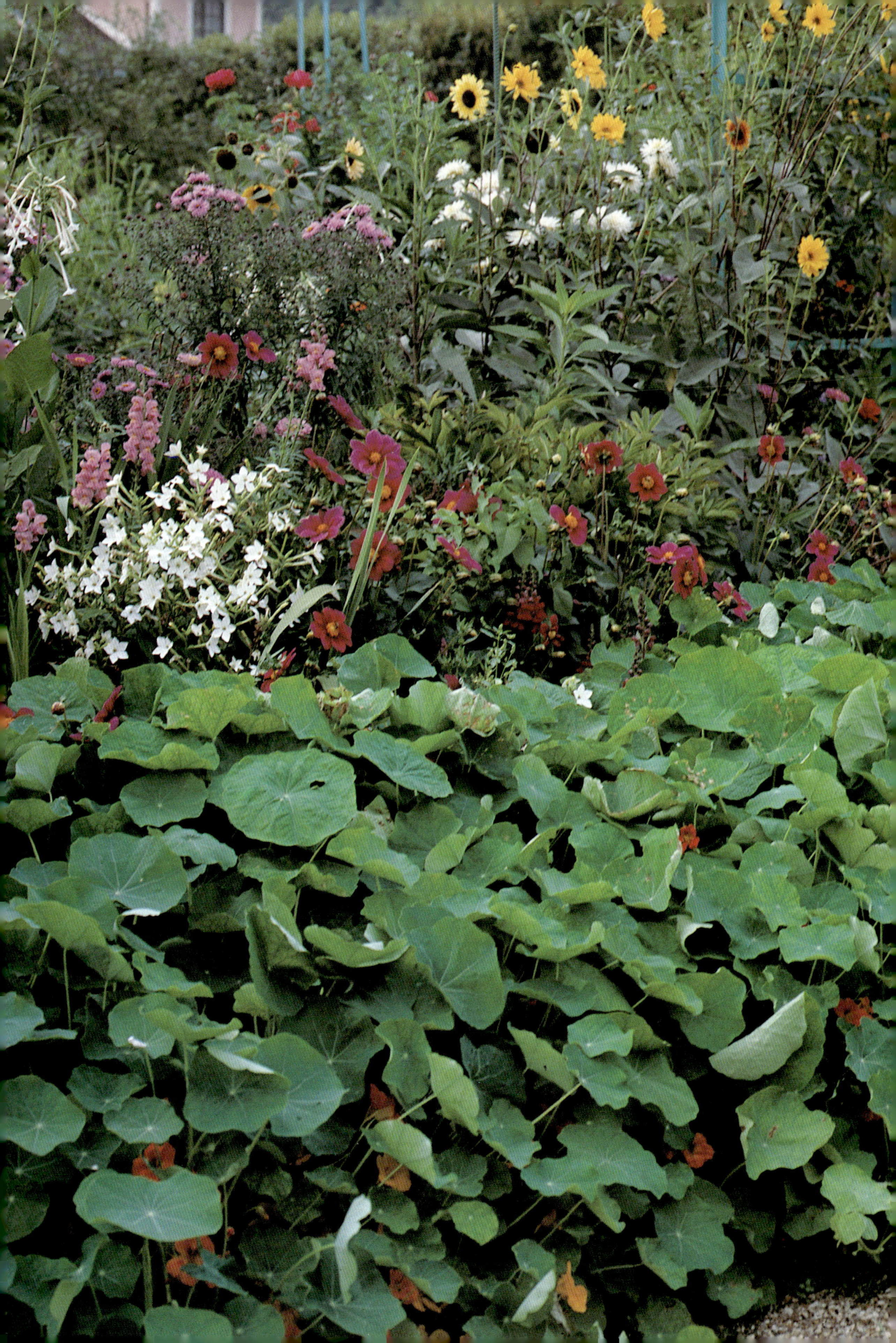

Edible Flowers

One usually associates flowers with visual pleasure, but many flowers also provide culinary delights. The presence of flowers in cooking may go beyond the conventional to introduce the unexpected or the exotic in both taste and appearance.

The beauty, colour and fragrance of flowers will improve the tone of an otherwise pedestrian table setting. The distinctive flavours of particular flowers encourage experimentation leading to new and appealing gourmet delights. Such experimentation is particularly applicable to cakes, desserts and salads. A cake with white icing, for example, can be turned into an elegant creation by adding several violet flowers and leaves. Salads can be varied and enhanced by the addition of a few carefully selected flowers. Flowers frozen in ice-cubes can be used as an attractive addition to summer drinks.

Flowers gathered for eating should be blemish-free and not sprayed with chemicals. Pick them early in the morning and wash them quickly in cool water to remove dust. Keep them fresh by placing them in the refrigerator in a bowl of water or a plastic bag.

The flowers of lavender, nasturtiums and violets impart flavour and fragrance when added to white wine vinegar and used as a salad dressing. The small, beautiful violet (*Viola odorata*), which in ancient times was the symbol of Athens and the flower of Aphrodite, also has other uses. Apart from the flower's widespread use in perfumes, flavourings and medicines, the leaves contain an abundant supply of vitamins C and A. It is a valued garden plant, thriving in shady areas under trees where it is often difficult for anything else to grow.

Pansies (*Viola x wittrockiana*) and violas (*Viola cornuta*) belong to the same genus as violets but flower after violets have finished.

Nasturtium leaves and flowers are colourful salad ingredients

These low-growing annuals exhibit deep, rich colours and their delicate taste and beauty make them a welcome addition to salads. Use colours which complement the salad ingredients. Picking pansy flowers will actually encourage more flowers to appear. Pansies are hardy, fast growing and thrive in full sun or dappled shade.

Old-fashioned daylilies (*Hemerocallis* species) are easy to grow and will adapt to full sun or dappled shade. Their large heads of buds appear in late spring and early summer and open every day into showy, trumpet-shaped flowers.

The complete, delicate-tasting flower should be added to food for a dramatic effect, or if you prefer, you can use the petals only. Flower colours include orange, lemon, pink and purple.

The common name for daisies was once 'measure of love' which derived from the well-known custom of using the flower as a love oracle. The oracle was performed by pulling off daisy petals and saying alternately 'he loves me, he loves me not'. As daisies usually have odd petals it was difficult to lose if one started off with 'he loves me'.

The contrast between the dark green leaves of spinach or silverbeet and the small, dainty light pink flowers of the English daisy (*Bellis perennis*) makes a visually arresting salad. Easily grown from seed planted in winter, established English daisies will readily self-seed. Given regular applications of plant food and plenty of water they will provide masses of flowers through spring and early summer. There is a bonus in that they will grow in partial shade.

The Latin words 'primula veris' mean 'first of spring' and the dainty flowers of this plant are aptly named. Polyanthus (*Primula x polyantha*) is the only species of this genus which can be eaten and the flowering period lasts for at least a month.

The name nasturtium means 'nose-twisting' and is derived from the Latin words 'nasus-tortus', which refers to the peppery taste of the plant. With a taste similar to watercress, the leaves and flowers add zest to sandwiches as well as salads. These remarkable plants will actually produce more flowers if they are grown in a poor soil. Too much plant food will cause an abundance of leaves to the detriment of the flowers. Trailing types are often used for groundcovers or are seen spilling over the sides of terracotta pots. Versatility is a major attraction with nasturtiums. In the vegetable garden they are natural companion plants to broccoli and

The pretty flowers of Bellis perennis *make a pleasing garnish*

Pansies may be used to decorate cakes and salads

radishes. Grown underneath apple trees they will deter woolly aphids.

Toss a few orange or yellow petals of pot marigolds (*Calendula officinalis*) through a salad to imbue it with an unusual but subtle taste. Pot marigolds also combine well with eggs or cottage cheese. Cutting the flowers back to a node on the stem will encourage another show of flowers.

The flowers of lavender and geraniums are well known ingredients in potpourris and sachets. When used with restraint they add a persuasive perfume to food, especially sweet desserts. The leaves of both species may also be used, but only sparingly.

Both the leaves and flowers of clover (*Trifolium* species), which is becoming a popular lawn alternative, can be eaten. The nutritious flowers should be added to spring salads, while the sweet tasting leaves may be eaten raw in sandwiches. Alternatively, they can be lightly steamed. The genus name *Trifolium* is derived from the trifoliate leaves, which are divided into three leaflets joined in the centre. Children love searching for the mutations of these leaves—the four-leafed clover. Red and white clover are the two most popular varieties. Red clover is recognised by its purplish or pink flowers, contrary to what the name suggests. White clover has creamy-white flowers.

The rose is said to 'keep its dignity even as it dies' which is true, as the dried petals are put to use in pot-pourris. Rose petals were used as filling in medieval tarts or were turned into jams. They add fragrance, colour and a delicate taste to many dishes. The rose-hips are used in teas and are extremely high in vitamin C. Any variety of rose may be used but the old-fashioned types have more taste and fragrance.

The leaves of dandelions (*Taraxacum officinale*) are delicious when mixed in a salad with a sweet fruit like rockmelon. The contrast between the bitterness of the dandelion and the sweetness of the rockmelon is superb.

The flowers of chives, pumkins and lavender may be used as a garnish

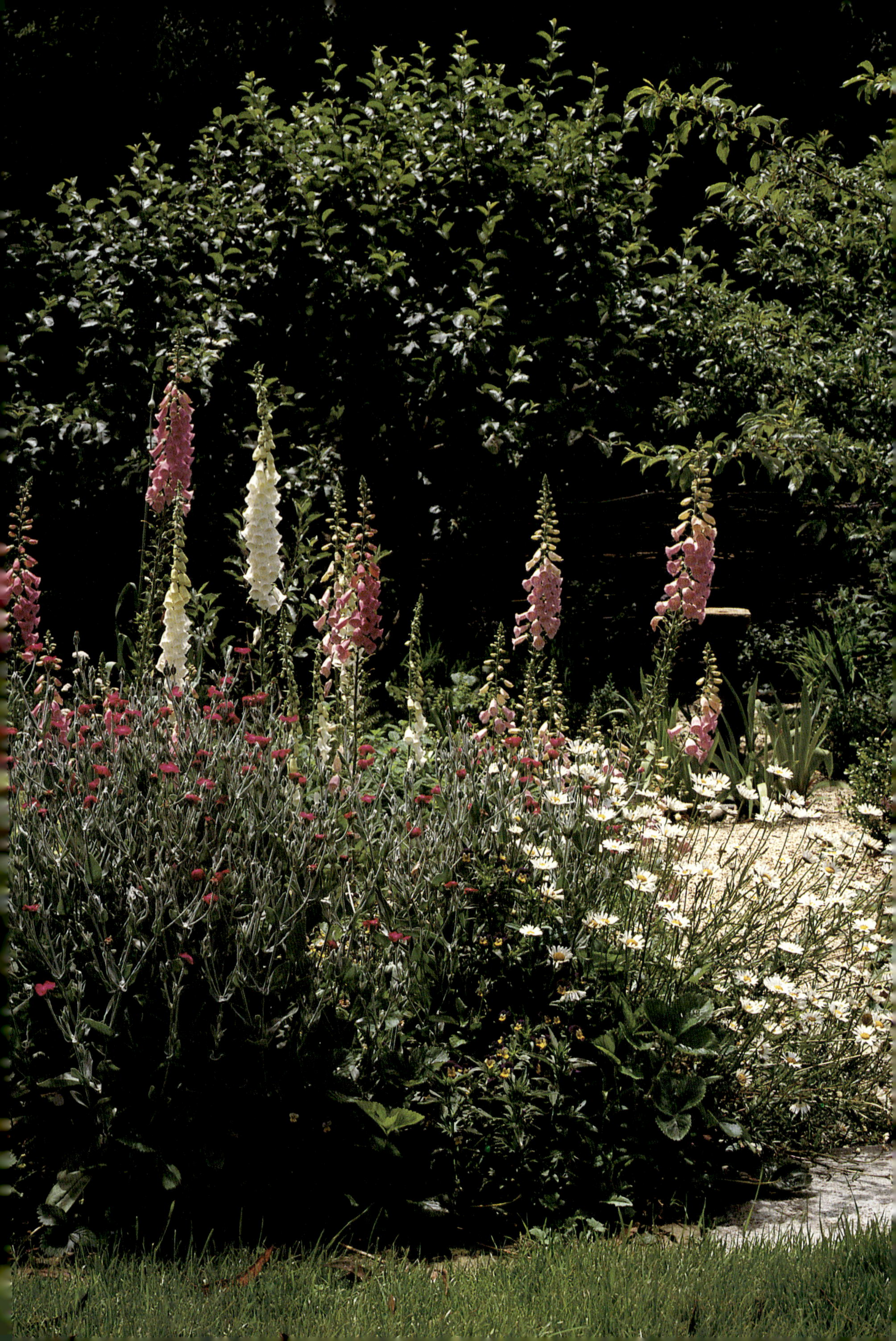

Soil Preparation

THE secret of success when growing any type of plant is to start with a rich, fertile soil. Taking the time and trouble to understand and prepare the soil initially will save hours of labour and reward you with healthy plants. Plants grown in good soil are less likely to be attacked by insects and diseases.

Improving Soil Structure

A good garden should have a topsoil that is at least a metre deep, is reasonably fertile and has a good balance of sand, silt and clay particles. It should have the right amount of air between these particles to promote both good drainage and water retention. It must also have a good acid/alkaline balance for healthy plant growth.

Sandy Soil

Sandy soil has its advantages as well as its disadvantages. The main disadvantage is that it drains too quickly and nutrients are lost with this free drainage. Sandy soil is easy to improve by adding plenty of organic matter like leaf mould, compost or animal manure. These will increase its water-holding capacity and will supply nutrients to the plants.

Loam

Most loam soils are easy to work and have good drainage. Adding organic matter into the soil provides nutrients which will be released slowly to plants.

Clay

A clay soil has its problems because it retains a high percentage of water. It needs to be watered less often than a sandy soil but it will restrict the normal penetration of the root system because of the slow movement of air

A rich soil will sustain a wealth of plants.

and the slow drainage. A clay soil can be balanced by adding large quantities of organic matter like compost, leaf mould or animal manure. Gypsum should also be added as it causes a coagulation of clay particles and this facilitates the drainage and movement of air through the soil.

There is a liquid product on the market called an organic claybreaker which, when watered into the soil, will break up the heavy clay. It is claimed that the claybreaker is totally organic and that the treatment will be effective within six to eight weeks of application. It need only be used every four years, but for best results the claybreaker should be used in conjunction with organic matter.

Lupins look pretty in the garden and are good for the soil

Soil pH

Soil pH is a measure of the amount of acidity or alkalinity in the soil. The pH of the soil can affect a plant's growth in the following ways: it has an effect on the availability of essential nutrients; it has an effect on soil micro-organisms; and it affects the roots' ability to absorb both water and nutrients.

The pH level of the soil is measured on a scale which runs from zero to fourteen. Zero is on the acid end and fourteen is on the alkaline end. At the middle of the scale, i.e. seven, the soil will be neutral. The soil can be tested by obtaining a pH soil-testing kit from garden centres or nurseries.

If you find that the soil is too acidic, this can be corrected easily by adding dolomite or lime. Wood ash is also beneficial to acidic soils. An alkaline soil can be corrected by adding organic matter such as peat, pine leaves or decayed oak leaves. Alternatively, use sulphate of aluminium or sulphate of iron at the rate of 2 tablespoons per square metre. Hydrangea blueing tonics and European peat moss also have an acidifying effect.

Building healthy soil

Composting is the traditional way of using waste organic material and one that is receiving increasing attention as individuals seek to adopt energy-efficient practices. But if you do not have the space for a compost heap there are various other organic materials that will enrich your soil.

Manure

Animal manures have been used for centuries to build healthy soil. The two most commonly used manures are cow and poultry but you can use horse, pig, goat, sheep or rabbit. Manure can be dug directly into the garden bed or used as a mulch in spring.

Mushroom compost

Mushroom compost is ideal for adding texture to the soil as it has been formed from a mixture of straw, manure and lime. Apply it as a mulch during spring or dig into the garden bed before planting out spring annuals and perennials.

Seaweed

Seaweed adds structure to soil as well as being a valuable source of plant food. It contains as much nitrogen, half the phosphorus and twice as much potassium as manure, as well as an enormous variety of trace elements, and powerful antibiotics. Between 20 and 50 per cent of some seaweeds are minerals. Hose the seaweed down before use to get rid of the salt. It can be dug directly into the ground when the garden bed is being prepared, or used as a mulch around plants. Because it is low in phosphorus, add some rock minerals or blood and bone.

Compost

Compost improves the structure, water-holding capacity and aeration of soils containing excessive amounts of clay or sand.

The range of suitable organic materials is considerable. All types of leaves, hay, waste vegetable matter, vegetable garden refuse, sawdust, wood wastes, grass clippings or any animal manures or weeds can be used. Many people do not add weeds for fear of the seeds being spread throughout the garden. They overlook the fact that a well made compost heap will reach an internal temperature of 42 degrees Centigrade, which will kill any weed seeds present.

Organic soil produces healthy plants

The ideal size for a compost heap is 1.25 m square and 1.5 m high. It can, of course, be larger or smaller depending on the size of the garden. One of the simplest and most effective methods of building a container involves using metal fencing poles and chicken wire. Four stakes are needed for a single heap and six stakes for two heaps. Only three sides of the structure need to be enclosed with chicken wire. The beauty of this type of container is that it allows free air circulation around it.

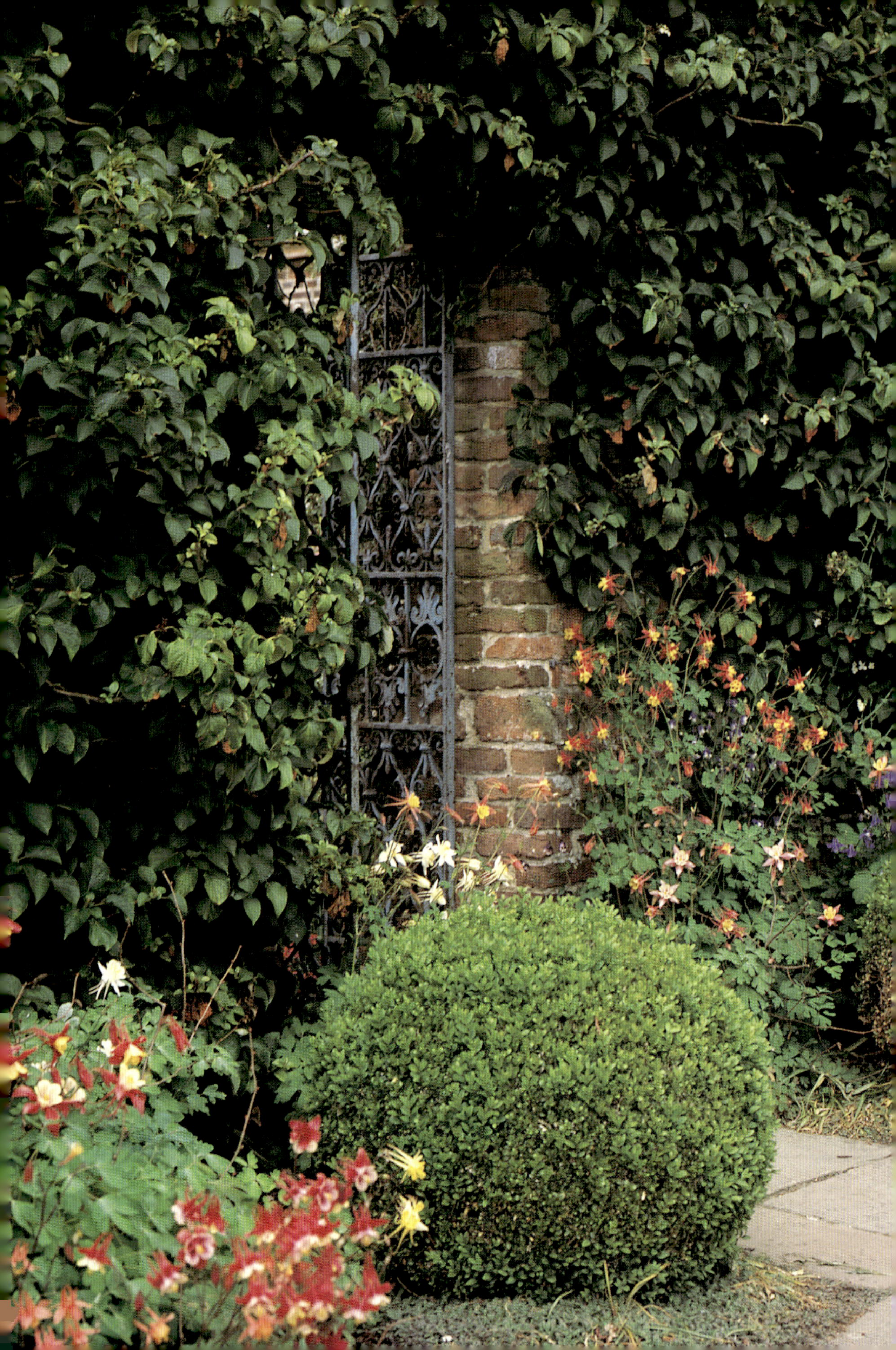

Maintenance

The growth of your annuals and perennials will depend entirely on how well they are planted initially and how well they are maintained. But with correct planting and feeding you will be well rewarded for your efforts.

Planting annuals

The best time to transplant annuals is on an overcast day or a day with light rain. This is not always possible, of course. The end of the day is better for planting than early morning, especially in summer when plants are subject to the hot sun during the day.

Add manure or compost to the bed before you commence planting annuals and make sure the soil is wet.

To thin out seedlings that you have sown directly in the garden, place a trowel under the clump of seedlings and carefully remove the clump. Pull the seedlings apart gently and transplant immediately.

Annuals that are to be transplanted from punnets should be thoroughly watered in their containers. A moist root-ball will not fall apart or stick to the edge of the container. Plant the seedlings slightly deeper than they were in the container and firm the soil around them with your hands.

Some wilting is natural immediately after planting so it is very important to keep the soil moist for a couple of days.

Planting perennials

A perennial will grow in the same spot for many years, so its initial planting is very important. If you are starting a new garden bed it is advisable to incorporate organic matter in the form of cow manure or compost into the soil before planting. Otherwise dig the hole for the perennial deeper than required, add manure or compost to the bottom of the hole, then cover with a little soil.

Regular feeding will ensure an abundance of flowers

The hole should always be dug several centimetres larger in diameter than the spread of the roots, as this will give the roots space to become established quickly. Fill in around the perennial with soil, taking care that it is planted at the proper depth, which is the same depth that it was in the pot.

Remember that the main goal in transplanting—whether you have a new plant or one obtained through division of an older plant—is to avoid shocking the plant excessively. Water it carefully before and after planting. Don't let roots dry out or break off as they are the plant's lifeline for food, moisture and good health.

Feeding

Annuals and perennials must be fed regularly to keep them growing steadily and free from pests and diseases.

There are two methods of feeding plants. You can use a commercial complete plant food or organic materials. A complete plant food is ideal because it has all the required elements for healthy growth. The best method of all is to combine a complete plant food with organic materials.

Plants require 16 elements to grow satisfactorily, three of which are the carbon, hydrogen and oxygen found in both air and water. The remaining 13 elements required are divided into two groups—major elements and minor, or trace, elements.

The major elements are: nitrogen, phosphorus, sulphur, potassium, magnesium and calcium.

The trace elements are: iron, manganese, boron, molybdenum, copper and zinc. Most of these elements are ever-present in the soil but the demands on nitrogen, phosphorus and potassium are such that they need to be replenished more regularly.

The lack of any of these three is recognisable and can be fixed simply by adding manure or compost. One of the best ways to gain an understanding of the major nutrient problems of your soil is to have it tested by using your own soil testing kit or by sending it to a laboratory.

Nitrogen is necessary for the growth of new tissue. A lack of nitrogen is easy to diagnose because plants appear stunted and have yellow or pale green leaves that seem thinner than normal. Manure is a good source of nitrogen. An overdose of nitrogen in the soil causes soft, sappy growth with profuse foliage but very few flowers.

Phosphorus is essential for strong, healthy growth and fruit development. It also helps plants to resist disease. Plants deficient in phosphorus will appear to be stunted, with poor root growth and little or no fruit. The leaves tend to become discoloured, turning purple, red or bluish green. Animal manures, blood and bone and wood ash are organic sources of phosphorus.

Potassium helps develop robust plants. It builds up the firm outer tissues and is responsible for richly coloured fruits. If the soil is deficient in this element, the plants will have virtually no resistance to heat, cold or disease and the process of photosynthesis will be greatly slowed. Organic sources of potassium include wood ash, straw and animal manures.

When to feed

Even if garden beds are regularly mulched with manure or compost it is helpful to add supplementary plant food, especially for annuals and perennials. An application of soluble plant food in early and late spring and early and late summer will give plants a boost. Soluble plant food usually improves flower size and quality if applied as flowering commences. It is also beneficial to scatter a handful of complete plant food over the soil when planting annuals or perennials.

When applying fertiliser, whether it be commercial liquid or commercial dry fertiliser, blood and bone, fish emulsion, seaweed emulsion or manure, always be sure to follow the directions on the package. Too much is usually more dangerous than not enough.

Liquid manure

Liquid manure is an ideal way to supply any

An organic mulch prevents weed growth and supplies food to plants

element, especially nitrogen, to a plant very quickly. Liquid manure is made easily by combining one-third manure and two-thirds water in a plastic bucket and letting it steep for about two weeks.

Mulching

Organic matter applied as a mulch feeds plants and improves soil texture. Apart from supplying food, an organic mulch performs three other important functions: it conserves moisture by reducing evaporation; it prevents weed growth by restricting light at the soil surface; and it modifies soil temperatures by cooling or warming the soil.

Organic mulches are biodegradable and earthworms accelerate the decay process. They thrive in the layer of soil just below the mulch, where they carry on their work of aerating and enriching the soil. Worms also carry broken-down bits of mulch below the surface, thereby increasing the amount of humus around the roots.

Mulching materials

Materials for a mulch usually consist of what you have on hand or whatever is readily available in your area. Cow or chicken manure and home-made compost are wonderful mulches when used by themselves or topped with grass clippings. Pinebark and sawdust, on the other hand, tend to take too much nitrogen out of the soil to the detriment of plants. If you must use them, apply a thick mulch of cow or chicken manure first.

Autumn leaves make a perfect mulch, especially if they have been shredded. They can be mixed with straw, manure or mushroom compost.

Watering

A garden that has been properly mulched and has a healthy soil full of organic matter is able to withstand a great deal of heat before it requires watering. An overwatered garden will weaken a plant's resistance because its roots will stay shallow. The roots of plants in a garden that has not been overwatered will go deeper into the earth looking for water. Unfortunately there are no hard and fast rules about when and how to water. It depends on the climate and the type of soil. The main point is to always water thoroughly so that the water seeps right down into the soil.

I have also observed that if a garden bed is heavily planted it does not dry out as quickly as one with a great deal of bare earth. A variety of annuals and perennials of different sizes will help to shade the earth and each other.

Annuals and perennials which are fed regularly will be free from pest and diseases

MAINTENANCE

This abundant planting leaves no room for weeds

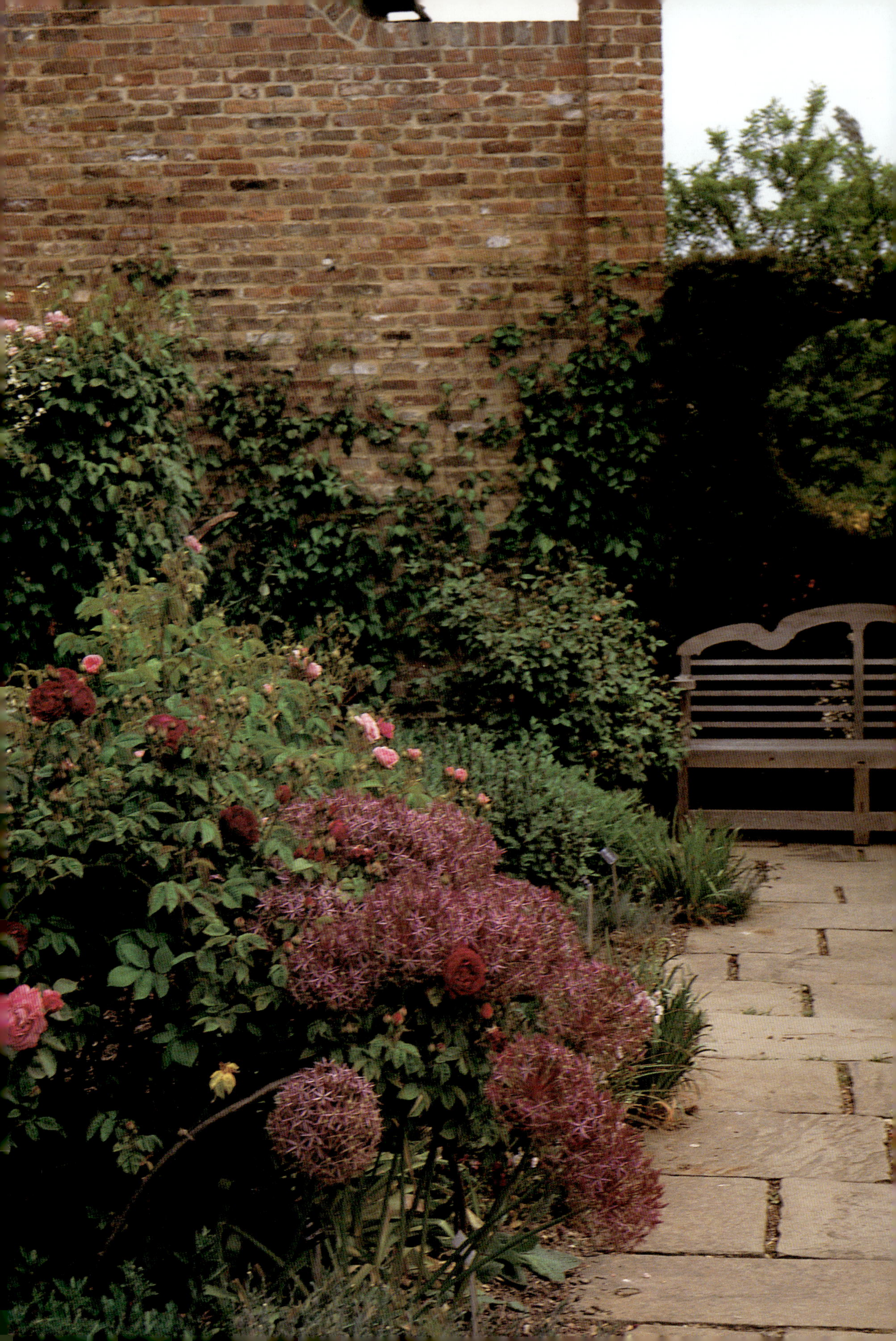

Propagation

The majority of perennials are propagated by division. After a few years growth, most perennials need dividing. This keeps the plant healthy as well as supplying you with extra plants to swap with friends or to replant in your garden. Division of perennials is carried out when the plant is going through its dormant stage or at the beginning of spring when new growth appears.

Dividing perennials

- Carefully remove the plant from the ground.
- Shake away some of the soil so that the roots are easily seen.
- The root ball can now be divided by pulling it apart with your hands, a spade, or a sharp knife.
- Replant the divisions immediately and keep well-watered until the new plants are established.
- The original clump can be either replanted or discarded, depending on its health.

Growing from seed

A seed is the product of a fertilised ovule, consisting of an embryo enclosed by a protective seed coat. It is a young, undeveloped plant with a food source.

The process of a seed sprouting roots and leaves is one of the great miracles of nature. Three conditions need to be met before germination occurs: adequate moisture, suitable temperature and sufficient air. Moisture is necessary to soften the seed coat and allow the embryo (the undeveloped plant) to expand and grow.

A suitable temperature is needed to break dormancy. Different seeds germinate at different temperatures.

Air is required for seeds to live. If the soil is waterlogged for an extended period or the seeds are started in a heavy potting mix, they will die. Because of this it is essential to have a

The majority of perennials need to be divided every three or four years

potting mix that drains well, so that air can enter the soil.

Many people choose to buy seedlings from a nursery rather than start their own plants. The main advantage of starting your own seeds is the large choice of varieties available. Selections of ready-grown seedlings are always limited to a few popular varieties.

Propagating cases

Propagating cases may be obtained from garden centres and nurseries. The simplest type is a transparent lid or dome that fits over a seed tray. Also available are cases which are similar to miniature greenhouses. These are made of plastic over a wire frame and can be used for seeds or cuttings.

Seed-raising mixtures

The mixture in which seeds are sown is very important. Seed-raising mixtures may be obtained from nurseries or garden centres. Choose one that contains vermiculite so that the mix will be open enough for the roots to penetrate easily and air to circulate. It should also hold water without becoming soggy. Seed-raising mixtures can be made at home by using the following ingredients:

---

1 part well-moistened and squeezed-out peat moss
4 parts vermiculite
4 parts coarse river sand

or

2 parts coarse river sand
1 part peat moss.

Seedlings raised in home-made mixes like the above need to be fed when the plants reach 2.5 cm in height, with a soluble plant food diluted to half its normal strength.

Sowing seeds

Press the seed-raising mixture down firmly to about 1 cm from the top of the tray. In most cases fine seed only needs to be pressed down into the surface of the mix. Larger seeds usually need a soil covering of twice their thickness. The depth is usually indicated on the seed packet.

It is essential that while the seed is germinating the mix should be kept moist but not too wet. The easiest method of ensuring this is to place a plastic or glass cover over the container to help retain the moisture. Additional water will not be necessary unless the seeds take longer than three weeks to germinate. Alternatively, place the seed trays in a propagating case or start them in a hotbed or coldframe. Do not water from overhead as the seeds might be washed into congested drifts. If watering is necessary place the tray in a larger container of water and let the seed-raising mixture soak up the moisture from below. Place the seed tray in strong, direct light but not direct sunlight.

Transplanting

After the seedlings have made their second or third leaves, either thin them or transplant them. Always water the seedlings prior to transplanting and make sure that the ground into which they will be transplanted is also damp. Thin by removing all but the most promising ones. Take care when removing a seedling from the container not to damage its roots. Lever it out of the container with a small, pointed tool. When placing the seedling in the ground make sure that the roots are not cramped, then replace the soil gently around it.

During the first week or so after transplanting keep the plants well watered to encourage steady growth.

Direct sowing

Large seeds that are easy to manage can be planted directly into the ground. This saves transplanting and avoids setbacks which may occur when young plants are moved. Always follow the directions on the packet as to the planting depth and distance apart. The soil that covers the seeds should be fine and not lumpy. A seed-raising mixture will give best results. Keep the ground moist after planting until the young seeds emerge from the ground.

Cuttings

Plants propagated vegetatively or asexually reproduce, by means of DNA replication, all the genetic information of the parent plant. This is why the unique characteristics of any single plant are perpetuated in the propagation of a clone. New plants can even be started from a single cell, as any living cell of a plant has all the genetic information needed to regenerate the complete organism.

In propagation by cuttings a piece of stem, root or leaf is cut from the parent plant, after which this piece is placed under certain favourable environmental conditions and induced to form roots and shoots. This produces a new independent plant which, in most cases, is identical to the parent plant.

Stem cuttings are the most common type of cutting and these can be divided into four groups according to the nature of the wood used in making the cuttings: hardwood, semi-hardwood, softwood and herbaceous. Perennials are propagated by softwood and herbaceous cuttings.

Propagating medium

The correct propagating medium will influence the number of cuttings that will root and the quality of the root system formed. A mixture of 2 parts river sand and 1 part peat moss is most effective.

Plant hormones

Plant hormones are applied to cuttings to encourage the production and even distribution of roots. Hormones also shorten the time taken by the plant to root. The end of the cutting is dipped into the powder before it is placed in the propagating medium.

Softwood cuttings

These types of cuttings are taken from either deciduous or evergreen plants. Take them during early spring when the growth is rapid and the stems are quite flexible. Softwood cuttings generally root more easily and more quickly than the other types but require more attention. The best softwood cutting material has some degree of flexibility, but is mature enough to break when bent sharply.

A glasshouse is an ideal place to start cuttings and seeds

Some of the best cutting material comes from the lateral or side branches of the stock plant. Cuttings should be 7.5-15 cm long, with two or more nodes and the basal cut made just below a node. The leaves on the lower portion of the cutting are removed, with those on the upper part retained. Large leaves can be cut in half.

Herbaceous cuttings

These are taken from succulent plants such as geraniums, chrysanthemums or coleus. Make the cutting 8-12 cm long and prepare in the same way as softwood cuttings.

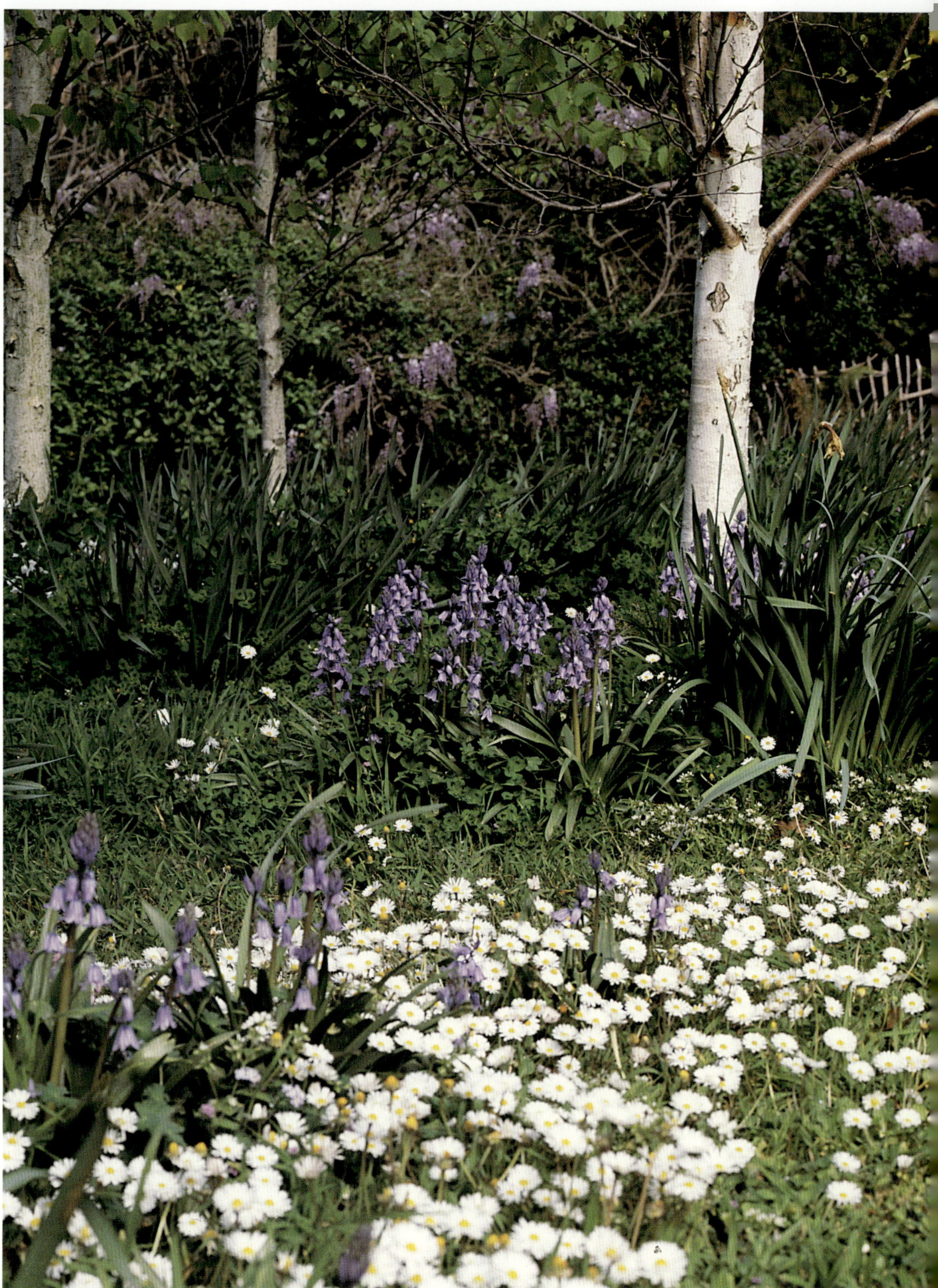

A lawn filled with self-sown Bellis perennis

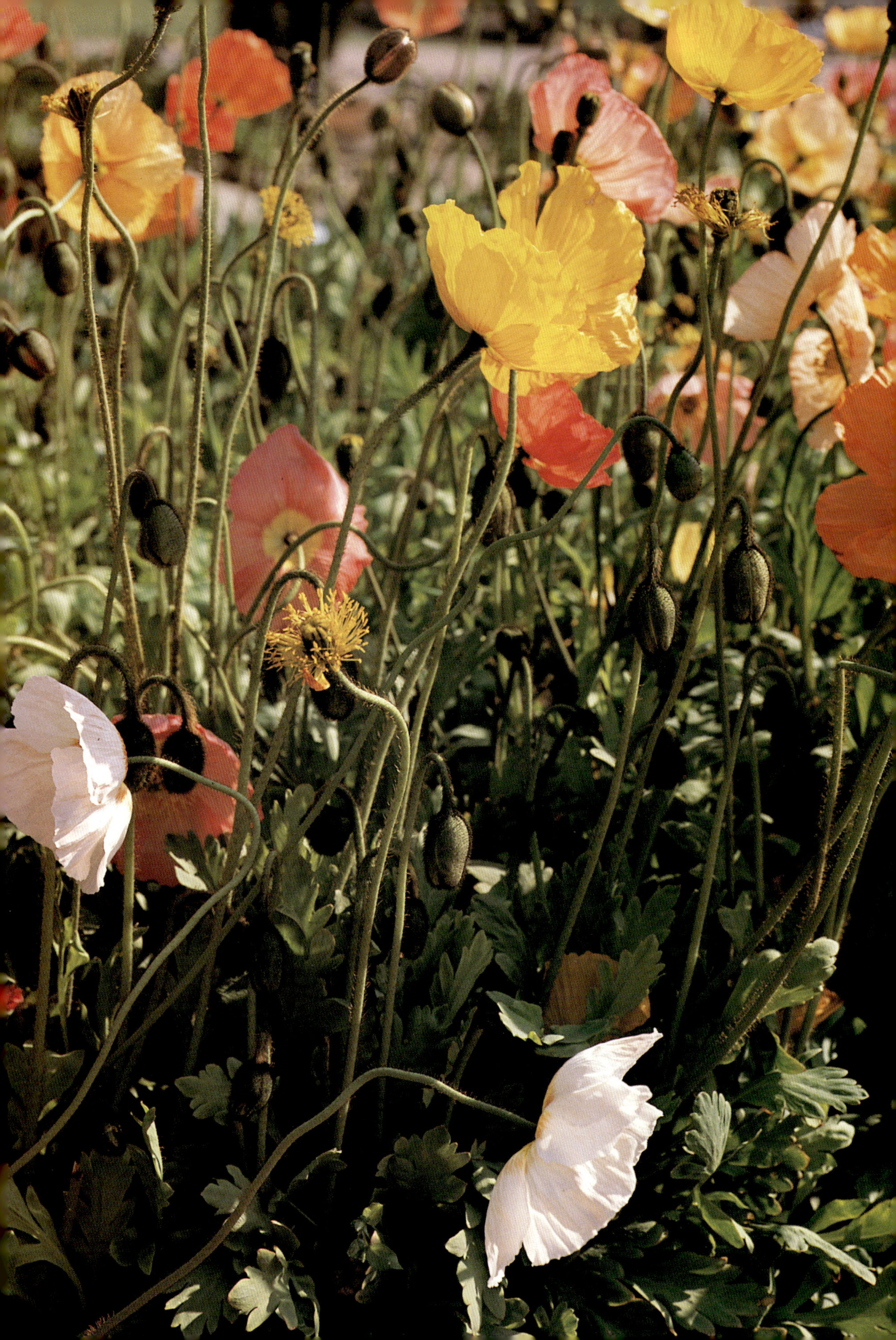

Annuals
A Selection List

Ageratum houstonianum (floss flower)
FLOWER COLOUR White and shades of blue
FLOWERING TIME Warm climates: throughout the year. Cold climates: summer and autumn
DESCRIPTION Grown for their spring, summer and autumn flowers which reach a height of aproximately 20 cm. Flowers appear for 3 months.
CULTIVATION A hardy annual which will grow in full sun or lightly dappled shade. Keep moist during summer.
PROPAGATION Seed can be sown in containers and transplanted or sown directly where it is to be grown.

Agrostemma githago 'Milas' (corn cockle)
FLOWER COLOUR Rosy purple
FLOWERING TIME Spring and summer
DESCRIPTION A pretty, quick-growing cottage garden annual having wiry stems, topped by five-petalled flowers with a tubular calyx.
CULTIVATION Corn cockle will thrive in any well-drained soil in full sun. It will readily self-seed.
PROPAGATION Sow the seed in autumn for spring flowers. The seed may be sown directly where it is going to grow.

Amaranthus caudatus (tassel-flower, love-lies-bleeding)
FLOWER COLOUR Red
FLOWERING TIME Late summer and autumn
DESCRIPTION A tall annual reaching a height of 1–2 m. It is widely grown for its red foliage and flowers and its ability to withstand hot weather.
CULTIVATION A sunny, dry position with protection from strong winds. Water frequently during hot weather.
PROPAGATION Sow directly where it is to grow in spring when danger of frost is over.
CULTIVARS 'Viridis' has yellowish green flowers.
OTHER SPECIES *A. hybridus* has red flowers and leaves.

Iceland poppy (Papaver nudicaule)

Queen Anne's lace (*Ammi majus*)

Ammi majus (Queen Anne's lace)
FLOWER COLOUR White
FLOWERING TIME Spring and summer
DESCRIPTION Heads of small white flowers. Reaches a height of 1–1.5 m. A good cottage garden plant.
CULTIVATION Full sun and shelter from wind.
PROPAGATION Seeds can be sown in containers and transplanted or sown directly where they are to grow.

Antirrhinum majus (snapdragon)
FLOWER COLOUR White, cream, pink, red, yellow or orange depending on the variety.
FLOWERING TIME Throughout the year
DESCRIPTION Old-fashioned annuals which carry many flowers along their main, and later their secondary, stems
CULTIVATION Place in full sun. Tip prune the plants when they are about 15 cm tall to produce bushier plants and more flowers.
PROPAGATION Sow seed in seed boxes or punnets and transplant to the garden when they are 5 cm high.
CULTIVARS 'Tetra Mixed' is a tetraploid strain 60 cm high with large ruffled flowers in shades of yellow, gold, rose, lilac, tango, deep red and white. 'Semi Dwarf Mixed' grows to 40–50 cm high and is suited for beddings and borders. 'Little Darling' is a compact bush and is available in a range of colours.

Calendula officinalis (English or pot marigold)
FLOWER COLOUR Shades of yellow and orange
FLOWERING TIME Late winter, spring and summer, depending on the sowing time.
DESCRIPTION Hardy plants that are popular because of their long flowering period.
CULTIVATION Full sun and a well-drained soil are the main requirements.
PROPAGATION Seed can be sown directly where it is to grow or raised in punnets.
CULTIVARS 'Campfire' is a semi-dwarf strain. Its orange flowers have a scarlet sheen. 'Pacific Beauty' has pastel shades of yellow, gold and orange. 'Honey Babe' is a dwarf variety. 'Princess Mixed' is a semi-dwarf strain with fully double blooms. Flowers are yellow, gold and orange.

Callistephus chinensis (Chinese aster)
FLOWER COLOUR Shades of pink, white, red, blue and purple
FLOWERING TIME Summer and autumn
CULTIVATION Full sun and protection from strong winds are their main requirements.
DESCRIPTION Popular annuals because of their rich, bright colours. Use in garden borders.
CULTIVATION Subject to aster wilt but will give good results if planted in soil which has not grown asters the previous year. Asters prefer a light sandy soil and a sunny position.
PROPAGATION Raise seedlings in punnets or seed beds and transplant when they are 5 cm high.
CULTIVARS 'Giant Crego Mixed' has large double flowers with long curled and twisted petals. 'King Aster' is popular for its double long-lasting flowers. 'Aster Mixed' is a good cut flower because of its large, evenly packed flower. 'Dwarf Colour Carpet' reaches a height of 20 cm. 'Bouquet' grows to about 40 cm, producing a profusion of pastel-coloured, pin-cushion-shaped blooms. 'Totem Pole' produces sturdy plants which are up to 60 cm tall. The fully double flowers have curled petals and a bright colour range.

Campanula medium (Canterbury bells)
FLOWER COLOUR White and shades of blue, lavender, pink and violet.
FLOWERING TIME Spring to summer
DESCRIPTION Grown for its beautiful, bell-shaped flowers which last for up to 9 weeks. Ideal for cottage gardens.
CULTIVATION Grow in sun or partial shade with protection from drying winds.
PROPAGATION Sow seed in punnets in autumn and transplant when they are 5 cm high, spaced 30 cm apart.

Celosia cristata (feathery amaranth or cockscomb)
FLOWER COLOUR Red, crimson, yellow or white
FLOWERING TIME Summer and autumn
DESCRIPTION Plumes of red flowers arise from green or red foliage
CULTIVATION Full sun and a well-drained soil.
PROPAGATION Seed can be sown directly where it is to grow or raised in punnets.
CULTIVARS 'Forest Fire' reaches a height of 90 cm and has scarlet plumes and contrasting dark foliage. 'Golden Triumph' has shimmering gold flowers. 'Fairy Fountains' is a dwarf variety with plumes in scarlet, salmon, light pink, gold and yellow.

CORNFLOWER (*CENTAUREA CYANUS*)

Centaurea cyanus (cornflower or bachelor's buttons)
FLOWER COLOUR Blue, white, pink, maroon or violet-blue
FLOWERING TIME Spring
DESCRIPTION Cottage garden favourites. Plant in drifts in the border. Reach a height of 75 cm and the multi-petalled daisy-like flowers are 4–5 cm wide.
CULTIVATION Full sun and a rich, organic, well-drained soil. Water regularly.
CULTIVARS 'Double Mixed' has a wide range of flower colours.

Cheiranthus cheiri (wallflower)
FLOWER COLOUR Orange, yellow, red, brown, crimson or white
FLOWERING TIME Spring
DESCRIPTION An old-world annual with a delightful fragrance. Useful for bedding or

CANTERBURY BELLS (*CAMPANULA MEDIUM*)

WHITE COSMOS (*COSMOS BIPINNATUS*) AND PINK ORIENTAL POPPIES

borders. Reaches a height of 60 cm.
CULTIVATION Grow in full sun and a well-drained soil. Give shelter from strong winds.
PROPAGATION Sow seed from mid-summer to autumn in punnets and transplant into the garden when they are 7 cm high.
CULTIVARS 'Russet Shades' produces large fragrant flowers in rich yellow, brown, mahogany, and deep ruby-red shades. 'Winter Delight' has double flowers.

Chrysanthemum coronarium (shungiku)
FLOWER COLOUR Golden yellow
FLOWERING TIME Summer and autumn
DESCRIPTION An easily-grown annual which reaches a height of 1 m. The leaves are sharply-toothed and divided. The young leaves are used in oriental dishes.
CULTIVATION Plant shungiku in well-drained soil and in a sunny position. It will readily self-seed throughout the garden.
PROPAGATION Sow the seed *in situ* in spring.

Clarkia amoena syn. *Godetia grandiflora* (godetia, satin flower)
FLOWER COLOUR Pink or white
FLOWERING TIME Summer
DESCRIPTION Hardy annuals having lance-shaped, mid-green leaves and 5-petalled, single or double flowers.
CULTIVATION Avoid over-rich soil as this encourages vegetative growth at the expense of flowers. Godetias like full sun and well-drained soil.
PROPAGATION Sow the seed directly where it is going to grow in autumn or early spring.

Cleome hasslerana (spider flower)
FLOWER COLOUR Rose-pink
FLOWERING TIME Summer and autumn
DESCRIPTION A tall annual which reaches a height of 2 m. The green leaves are aromatic and sticky. The unusual flowers have a spider-like appearance.
CULTIVATION Spider flower thrives in a sunny

position and well-drained, rich soil.
PROPAGATION Sow the seed in spring.

Consolida ambigua syn. *Delphinium ajacis* (larkspur)
FLOWER COLOUR Blue, pink, violet or white
FLOWERING TIME Spring
DESCRIPTION Dainty plants with tall slender stems and racemes of blue, lavender, white, pink or rose spring flowers. The foliage has a fine, delicate appearance.
CULTIVATION Grow in sun or partial shade with protection from winds. Fertilise monthly with a complete fertiliser until flowering begins. Mulch around the plants with grass clippings or manure. Snails and slugs can be a problem.
PROPAGATION Sow seeds in punnets and transplant when they are 5 cm high.
CULTIVARS 'Rainbow Mixed' is a hybrid selection in a variety of colours.
OTHER SPECIES *C. regalis* reaches a height of 1.2 m and bears large racemes of deep blue, pink or white spurred flowers in summer.

Cosmos bipinnatus (cosmos)
FLOWER COLOUR Red, white, yellow or pink with yellow centres
FLOWERING TIME Spring to summer
DESCRIPTION Tall annuals which are exceptional for background plants. The daisy-like flowers make excellent cut flowers.
CULTIVATION Full sun and shelter from strong winds. Cosmos is tolerant of most soil types but prefers a well-drained soil.
PROPAGATION Sow seeds directly in clumps in the garden and thin to the strongest seedlings or raise seedlings in punnets and transplant when they are 5 cm high.
CULTIVARS 'Mammoth Single Mixed' has rose and crimson flowers with a few white. 'Sunny Gold' is valued for its yellow double flowers.

Cynoglossum amabile (Chinese forget-me-not)
FLOWER COLOUR Blue
FLOWERING TIME Spring and summer
DESCRIPTION A quick-growing annual which reaches a height of 40 cm. From the oblong basal leaves arises a spike of brilliant blue forget-me-not-like flowers.

CULTIVATION An easily grown plant that will thrive in full sun or partial shade. It will readily self-seed throughout the garden.
PROPAGATION Sow the seed directly where it is to grow in spring.
OTHER SPECIES *C. officinale* has small, reddish purple flowers.

Dianthus barbatus (sweet William)
FLOWER COLOUR Red, mauve or pink marked with contrasting shades of these colours
FLOWERING TIME Spring to summer
DESCRIPTION A biennial plant that is usually treated as an annual. The carnation-like flowers are produced in abundance. Use in the border in drift or clumps.
CULTIVATION Plant in a sunny position and well-drained soil. If it is cut back in autumn it will return the following year.
PROPAGATION Sow seed in punnets in autumn or spring.

Dianthus chinensis (Chinese or Indian pink)
FLOWER COLOUR White, pink, red or lavender
FLOWERING TIME Late winter and spring
DESCRIPTION Pretty biennial plants with grey-green foliage and a mass of small, scented, carnation-like flowers. Colour range includes white and shades of pink, red and lavender. Overall height is 35 cm.
CULTIVATION Full sun and a well-drained soil.
PROPAGATION Sow seed in autumn or spring in punnets.
CULTIVARS There are many different varieties having single or double flowers often splashed or marked with concentric rings of contrasting colour.

Eschscholzia californica (Californian poppy)
FLOWER COLOUR Yellow, orange, scarlet or white
FLOWERING TIME Spring to late autumn
DESCRIPTION Pretty self-seeding annual plants with grey-green, lace-like foliage. Plant in drifts. Californian poppy self-seeds freely throughout the garden.
CULTIVATION Full sun and a well-drained soil.
PROPAGATION Sow seed directly into the garden bed in spring and summer.

CREAM CALIFORNIAN POPPIES (*ESCHSCHOLZIA CALIFORNICA*)

SWEET WILLIAM (*DIANTHUS BARBATUS*)
AND WHITE LYCHNIS

Alternatively, raise the seed in punnets and transplant into the garden when 5 cm high.

Geranium robertianum (herb Robert)
FLOWER COLOUR Pink
FLOWERING TIME Late spring to autumn
DESCRIPTION A delicate annual which reaches a height of 20 cm. The dainty green leaves turn red with age. Herb Robert is a hardy plant which makes a pretty groundcover. It will self-seed readily throughout the garden.
CULTIVATION Grow herb Robert in full sun or partial shade.
PROPAGATION Sow seed in early spring.

Gilia capitata (blue thimble flower)
FLOWER COLOUR Lavender blue
FLOWERING TIME Summer and autumn
DESCRIPTION A delicate annual which reaches a height of 80 cm. The tiny tubular flowers sit above the finely-pinnate leaves.
CULTIVATION Plant in a rich, organic soil in a sunny position.

PROPAGATION Sow seeds in spring.
OTHER SPECIES *G. tricolor* has a bushier habit and light blue flowers which are rimmed with violet.

Gomphrena globosa (globe amaranth)
FLOWER COLOUR Magenta-purple, violet pink or white depending on the cultivar.
FLOWERING TIME Mid-summer to late autumn
DESCRIPTION An attractive summer-flowering annual which reaches a height of 30 cm.
CULTIVATION Full sun and a well-drained soil. Add a complete fertiliser to the soil before planting. Keep the plants well-watered.
PROPAGATION Sow seeds in spring or early summer in punnets and transplant to the garden when they are 5–7 cm high.
CULTIVARS 'Little Buddy' has masses of purple, globe-shaped flowers.

Gypsophila elegans (baby's breath)
FLOWER COLOUR White, pink or carmine
FLOWERING TIME Throughout the year
DESCRIPTION Dainty clusters of tiny, single or double flowers are carried above grey-green foliage in spring and summer.
CULTIVATION Full sun and shelter from strong winds.
PROPAGATION Easily grown from seed, flowering 8–10 weeks after sowing. Sow seed directly into the garden, either in rows or in clumps. Thinning the seedlings is rarely necessary as plants flower well when spaced together.

Helianthus annuus (annual sunflower)
FLOWER COLOUR Yellow
FLOWERING TIME Summer
DESCRIPTION Grown for its stunning large flowers. Grow in clumps through the border for a spectacular display.
CULTIVATION Sunflowers prefer a sunny position, well-drained soil and shelter from wind. The taller varieties require staking. Protection from snails is necessary when the plants are young.
PROPAGATION Sow seed in spring.

Helichrysum bracteatum (strawflower)
FLOWER COLOUR White, yellow, orange, tan, rose-pink or red
FLOWERING TIME Early spring to late summer
DESCRIPTION The pretty, papery, daisy-like blooms are excellent for cutting and drying.
CULTIVATION Well-drained soil and a sunny position. Ideal for dry inland areas. Add complete fertiliser to the bed before planting.
PROPAGATION Sow seed in punnets in spring.

Helipterum manglesii (everlasting strawflower)
FLOWER COLOUR Pink
FLOWERING TIME Summer
DESCRIPTION The glossy, pink bracts give the flower a straw-like appearance. The flowers are excellent for drying.
CULTIVATION Strawflower requires a sunny position and well-drained soil.
PROPAGATION Sow the seed directly into the soil in spring.
CULTIVARS 'Maculatum' has brighter coloured pink flowers.
OTHER SPECIES *H. humboldtianum* has white, woolly leaves and yellow flowers. *H. roseum* has pink or white flowers with golden centres.

Hunnemannia fumariifolia (tulip poppy)
FLOWER COLOUR Yellow or white
FLOWERING TIME Summer and autumn
DESCRIPTION The tulip poppy has glaucous, grey foliage and slender flower stems.
CULTIVATION Plant in full sun and well-drained soil. Protection from wind is essential.
PROPAGATION Sow seed in spring.

Iberis umbellata (common annual or globe candytuft)
FLOWER COLOUR Mauve, lilac, pink, purple, carmine or white.
FLOWERING TIME Late spring to early autumn
DESCRIPTION A good bedding plant for borders.
CULTIVATION Requires a warm sunny position. Keep the ground damp.
PROPAGATION Sow seeds in spring in punnets and transplant to garden beds when they are 5 cm high.
OTHER SPECIES *I. amara* has white, scented summer and autumn flowers.

Impatiens balsamina (balsam)
FLOWER COLOUR Wide range of colours
FLOWERING TIME Spring to summer
DESCRIPTION Fleshy, shrub-like annual plants,

TALL SUNFLOWERS ARE OUTSTANDING PLANTS WHEN USED AT THE BACK OF A BORDER

A BLOCK OF CANDYTUFT (*IBERIS UMBELLATA*) IS AN EXQUISITE SIGHT

30–65 cm tall that self-seed freely through the garden. The foliage is a bright green.
CULTIVATION A position in full sun or semi-shade and a well-drained soil are the main requirements.
PROPAGATION Sow seed in punnets in autumn or spring.
CULTIVARS 'Superb Double Mixed' is a mixture of colours.

Impatiens wallerana (busy Lizzie)
FLOWER COLOUR Crimson, red, orange, pink, lavender or white
FLOWERING TIME Late spring to late autumn
DESCRIPTION A close relative of balsam but the plants are less compact and bear single flowers.
CULTIVATION A hardy plant that will thrive in poor conditions, sun or semi-shade. Readily self-seeds. Water regularly.
PROPAGATION Sow seeds in punnets in autumn and transplant to the garden when 5–7 cm tall.
CULTIVARS 'Baby Mixed' has a good range of flower colours.

Lathyrus odoratus (sweet pea)
FLOWER COLOUR All colours except yellow
FLOWERING TIME Late winter and early spring
DESCRIPTION Grown for their pea-shaped, perfumed flowers. Most are climbers but there are some bushy varieties.
CULTIVATION A sunny position and a well-drained soil with a pH of 6.5–7.0 are essential. Add animal manure or compost to the soil before planting. Water regularly. Cut spindly plants back lightly to encourage a more bushy growth.
PROPAGATION In temperate climates seed can be sown from mid-summer to late autumn, but March/April are the best months. In cold districts, spring sowings can be made. Sow the seed directly where it is to grow in shallow drills 2–3 cm deep and press the seeds into the soil 5–7 cm apart. If the soil is wet when sown, additional watering is usually unnecessary until seedlings emerge in 10–14 days. In very dry soil additional watering may be necessary while waiting for germination.

Lavatera trimestris (annual mallow)
FLOWER COLOUR White or pink
FLOWERING TIME Summer
DESCRIPTION A beautiful tall annual for the back of the border. It has branching stems and rounded, downy leaves. The flowers are trumpet-shaped.
CULTIVATION Annual mallow will grow in any well-drained soil and sunny position.
PROPAGATION Sow the seeds in spring directly where they are to grow.
CULTIVARS 'Silver Cup' has silvery pink flowers. 'Mt. Blanc' is a dwarf variety with white flowers. 'Loveliness' produces deep rose flowers.

Limonium sinuatum (annual statice)
FLOWER COLOUR Yellow, pink, blue or purple
FLOWERING TIME Summer and autumn
DESCRIPTION Annual statice is a biennial plant which is generally grown as an annual. The flowers are used in dried arrangements.
CULTIVATION Annual statice wil thrive in well-drained soil and full sun. It is very tolerant of dry conditions.
PROPAGATION Sow seeds in autumn in punnets and transplant to the garden when they are 7.5 cm high.

Linaria maroccana (toadflax)
FLOWER COLOUR Violet-purple, blue, pink, white or yellow
FLOWERING TIME Winter and spring
DESCRIPTION Colourful annuals which reach a height of 30–40 cm with spikes of flowers like tiny snapdragons.
CULTIVATION Full sun and a neutral soil are the main requirements. Add lime to the soil before planting if the soil is acidic.
PROPAGATION Sow seeds directly where they are to grow in clumps 10–15 cm apart. Thinning is usually unnecessary.
CULTIVARS *L. reticulata* reaches a height of 1.2 m and has yellow flowers.

Lobelia erinus (edging lobelia)
FLOWER COLOUR Blue-violet colour range and white
FLOWERING TIME Late winter, spring and summer
DESCRIPTION A dwarf, spring-flowering annual which is excellent for massed colour effect in garden beds.
CULTIVATION Full sun and a well-drained soil will produce an abundance of flowers.
PROPAGATION Sow seed in autumn or spring in punnets and transplant when 2–3 cm high.
CULTIVARS 'Crystal Palace' has bronze-green foliage and rich, dark blue flowers. 'String of Pearls' reaches a height of 15 cm and flowers in shades of pink, mauve and rose-purple. 'Basket Lobelia' has trailing stems up to 30 cm in length, bright green leaves and rich blue flowers with a white eye.

Lobularia maritima (alyssum, sweet alyssum)
FLOWER COLOUR White, lilac, pink or violet
FLOWERING TIME Late winter and spring
DESCRIPTION Pretty white, purple or rose flowers cover the grey-green foliage for virtually the whole year.
CULTIVATION Thrives in any soil in full sun or dappled shade. Lobularia self-seeds readily.
PROPAGATION Sow seed in early spring in punnets and transplant to the garden when 3 cm high.
CULTIVARS 'Carpet of Snow' has masses of pure white flowers. 'Royal Carpet' produces masses of deep purple flowers. 'Wonderland' forms attractive mounds with rose-pink flowers. 'Cameo Mixture' has a variety of colours.

Lunaria annua (honesty, money plant)
FLOWER COLOUR Violet-purple or white
FLOWERING TIME Summer and early autumn
DESCRIPTION The purple or white spring flowers are followed by circular, papery seed pods which are prized for flower decorations.
CULTIVATION Suitable for a sunny or shaded situation. Readily self-seeds.
PROPAGATION Sow the seed directly where it is to grow in early spring. Thin to 8–10 cm apart.

Lupinus hartwegii (annual lupin)
FLOWER COLOUR Blue, white, mauve or pink
FLOWERING TIME Summer
DESCRIPTION The pea-like flowers are borne on generous spikes against grey-green foliage.
CULTIVATION Lupins like a well-drained,

STOCK (*MATHIOLA INCANA*)

friable soil and a sunny position. Add lime to the soil before planting.
PROPAGATION Sow the seed directly where it is to grow. If the soil is dark and damp at the time of sowing, the seeds will germinate quickly. Too much moisture in the early stages can prevent germination.
CULTIVARS 'Pixie' is a dwarf variety 15–20 cm high.
OTHER SPECIES *L. densiflorus* reaches a height of 40 cm and has white, yellow or purple flowers.

Malcolmia maritima (Virginia stock)
FLOWER COLOUR Mauve, pink, white or cream
FLOWERING TIME Spring and summer
DESCRIPTION A dainty annual reaching a height of 20 cm. Excellent for edging or borders.
CULTIVATION Grow in full sun or partial shade in a friable, fertile garden soil.
PROPAGATION Sow seed directly where it is to grow in autumn. In cold climates sow in autumn and spring. Thinning is rarely necessary.

Mathiola incana (stock)
FLOWER COLOUR Most colours
FLOWERING TIME Spring
DESCRIPTION A popular spring flowering annual valued for its delicately fragrant flowers and grey foliage. Dwarf and tall varieties are available.
CULTIVATION Likes a neutral or slightly acid soil enriched with animal manure or compost. Plant in full sun with protection from strong winds. Stocks should be kept mulched to avoid moisture loss.
PROPAGATION Sow seeds from mid-summer to autumn in cold and temperate climates and autumn in hot climates. Seeds should be sown in punnets and transplanted to the garden when 7 cm high.
CULTIVARS Numerous varieties are available with heights ranging from 30–75 cm.
OTHER SPECIES *M. longipetala* (syn. *M. bicornis*) has dark pink flowers and is commonly called the night-blooming stock.

Molucella laevis (bells of Ireland, shell flower)
FLOWER COLOUR Green and white
FLOWERING TIME Summer
DESCRIPTION A tall annual reaching a height of 60 cm. Its shell-like green 'flowers' (really calyces) cover the stem in summer and autumn and are suitable for dried flower arrangements.
CULTIVATION Full sun and a well-drained soil are shell flower's main requirements. Self-seeds freely.
PROPAGATION Sow the seed in spring directly where it is to grow.

Myosotis sylvatica (forget-me-nots)
FLOWER COLOUR Blue
FLOWERING TIME Late winter and early spring
DESCRIPTION A hardy, self-seeding annual ideal for borders or use as a groundcover. The small flowers appear for up to 10 weeks.
CULTIVATION Can be grown in shade or dappled sunlight. An open, friable soil is ideal but the plants are adaptable and will adapt to most soil types.
PROPAGATION Sow the seeds directly where they are to grow and keep moist during the germination period (21–28 days). They may

FORGET-ME-NOTS (*MYOSOTIS SYLVATICA*) FORM A PRETTY GROUNDCOVER

be thinned out or left to grow close together.
CULTIVARS 'Alba' has white flowers. 'Rosea' is a dwarf form having pink flowers. 'Fisheri' has blue-pink flowers.

Nemesia strumosa (annual nemesia)
FLOWER COLOUR White, cream, yellow, orange, red, scarlet, crimson, blue or purple.
FLOWERING TIME Late winter and early spring
DESCRIPTION A colourful annual ideal for bedding or drifts through the garden.
CULTIVATION Plant in a mildly acidic or neutral soil. Prefers full sun. Nemesia will adapt to heavy or light soil. For bushier plants, pinch out the leading stem. Water regularly.
PROPAGATION Sow the seeds in early autumn in warm areas and in early spring in cool areas.
CULTIVARS 'Carnival Mixture' is a dwarf variety. 'Blue Gem' only reaches a height of 20 cm and has clear, sky-blue flowers.

Nemophila menziesii (baby blue eyes)
FLOWER COLOUR Blue
FLOWERING TIME Late winter and spring
DESCRIPTION A delightful annual reaching a height of 20–30 cm with fern-like foliage and small saucer-shaped flowers.
CULTIVATION Full sun or partial shade in hot areas. Baby blue eyes prefers a friable, fertile soil.
PROPAGATION Sow the seed in spring directly where it is to grow.
OTHER SPECIES *N. maculata* has white flowers with a purple spot at the tip of each lobe.

Nicotiana alata (tobacco plant)
FLOWER COLOUR White, mauve, purple, pink or lime-green
FLOWERING TIME Summer to autumn
DESCRIPTION Grown for its heady evening scent, tobacco plant can reach a height of 1.5 m and has large soft-green leaves. This species is actuallly a perennial but is generally treated as an annual.
CULTIVATION Full sun or partial shade in hot areas. Protection from wind and a fertile, well-drained soil enriched with organic matter are its main requirements. Cutting it back

THE FLOWERS OF NICOTIANA HAVE A
DELICATE PERFUME

after the flowering period will encourage more flowers. Tobacco plant will readily self-seed throughout the garden
PROPAGATION Sow the seed directly where it is to grow in spring.
CULTIVARS 'Lime Green' has green flowers. 'Rubella' produces beautiful deep red flowers.
'Grandiflora' has large, white flowers.
OTHER SPECIES *N. sylvestris* bears racemes of long, white, tubular flowers in spring and summer.

Nigella damascena (love-in-a-mist)
FLOWER COLOUR Blue, pink or white
FLOWERING TIME Spring
DESCRIPTION The pretty flowers are carried on top of the very fine, wispy foliage. The seed pods are valued for dried arrangements.
CULTIVATION Grow in full sun or partial shade. Water regularly. Love-in-a-mist self-seeds readily through the garden.
PROPAGATION Sow the seeds in succession from early spring *in situ* and thin out to 15 cm apart.

Papaver nudicaule (Iceland poppy)
FLOWER COLOUR Red, orange, yellow, pink or white
FLOWERING TIME Winter to early spring
DESCRIPTION The saucer-shaped flowers are carried on long stems above deeply lobed grey-green foliage.
CULTIVATION Full sun and a well-drained soil are essential. Picking the spent flowerheads will encourage more flowers to appear.
PROPAGATION Sow the seed thinly in punnets and cover with a light scattering of seed-raising mixture. Prick out the seedlings when they are 3–5 cm high and transplant to seedling boxes. Plant out in the garden when they are a good size, spacing the plants 20 cm apart.
CULTIVARS 'Artist's Glory' produces strong-stemmed flowers for a long period. 'Sunglow' has predominantly red, gold and orange flowers as well as pastel colours. 'Springsong' has large flowers and a wide colour range.

Papaver rhoeas (Flanders poppy)
FLOWER COLOUR Scarlet
FLOWERING TIME Late spring to summer
DESCRIPTION A slender annual which has soft green leaves. The scarlet flowers have a black blotch in the centre.
CULTIVATION A sun-loving plant which likes a cold climate and fairly dry soil.
PROPAGATION Sow the seed directly where it is going to grow in early spring.
CULTIVARS 'Shirley poppy' has single or double flowers in shades of red, pink and white.

Papaver somniferum (opium poppy)
FLOWER COLOUR Pink or red
FLOWERING TIME Spring and summer
DESCRIPTION The seed of the opium poppy is restricted commercially, but the double-flowering form, peony poppy, is often called *P. paeoniflorum*. This robust annual has large grey-green leaves. The seed pod looks just as handsome as the flowers.
CULTIVATION Plant in full sun and well-drained soil for good results.
PROPAGATION Sow the seed in spring directly where it is to grow.

Petunia x hybrida
FLOWER COLOUR Most colours including bicolours.
FLOWERING TIME Summer and early autumn
DESCRIPTION The flowers may be small or large, single or double with frilled or ruffled petals. The soft, hairy foliage is grey-green.
CULTIVATION Well-drained soil and a sunny position.
PROPAGATION Sow the seeds in punnets on the surface of the seed-raising mixture. Cover lightly with seed-raising mixture. Plant out into the garden when they are 5 cm high.
CULTIVARS There are many different varieties in a range of flower colours.

Phacelia campanularia (Californian bluebell)
FLOWER COLOUR Blue
FLOWERING TIME Summer
DESCRIPTION A hardy plant having grey-green leaves and slender stems which bear upturned bell-shaped, gentian blue flowers with yellow stamens. Reaches a height of 20 cm.
CULTIVATION Californian bluebell prefers a position in full sun or semi-shade. The soil should be light and well drained.
PROPAGATION Sow seed in spring.

Phlox drummondii (annual phlox)
FLOWER COLOUR Wide colour range
FLOWERING TIME Summer and autumn
DESCRIPTION Grown for their pretty flowers which are born in dense cymes on a neat, rounded head.
CULTIVATION Phlox prefer full sun but will grow in any position that has sun for part of the day. Pinch out plants when they are 10 cm high to make them more bushy.
PROPAGATION Sow the seed directly where it is to grow.
CULTIVARS 'Drummondii Dwarf' is a low-growing variety. 'Bright Eyes Mixture' is a taller strain reaching a height of 30–40 cm. The flowers have a white or contrasting centre. 'Twinkle Mixture' is a free-flowering dwarf mixture. The flowers are star-shaped. 'Derwent Dwarf Mixed' has a bushy habit and large flowers.

Primula malacoides (fairy primula)
FLOWER COLOUR Mauve, purple, pink, red, white or carmine
FLOWERING TIME Winter and early spring
DESCRIPTION The dainty flowers are carried above low, dense rosettes of pale green foliage.
CULTIVATION Flowers abundantly in sun or semi-shade. The soil should be neutral or slightly acidic.
PROPAGATION Sow the seeds in punnets on the surface and barely cover with seed-raising mixture. Transplant to the garden when the seedlings are 5 cm high.
CULTIVARS 'Carmine Glow' is a vigorous variety with carmine-rose flowers. 'Gillhams White' as the name suggests has white flowers. 'Royalty' has pink flowers and prefers semi-shade. 'Lollipops' is a dwarf primula.

Reseda odorata (mignonette)
FLOWER COLOUR Shades of red and yellow
FLOWERING TIME Winter and spring
DESCRIPTION An old-fashioned favourite valued for its small orange-yellow flowers which have a spicy aroma. Suitable for low borders or containers.
CULTIVATION A rich, well-drained soil in an open, sunny position. Add lime before planting if the soil is acidic.
PROPAGATION Sow the seed in autumn, winter and spring in temperate climates and autumn and spring in cold climates. Seeds can be planted directly where they are to grow.

Salpiglossis sinuata (painted tongue)
FLOWER COLOUR Shades of gold, bronze, red and violet.
FLOWERING TIME Spring and summer
DESCRIPTION A delightful plant for the back of a border. The trumpet-shaped flowers are 5 cm long.
CULTIVATION Full sun with protection from strong winds and a rich, friable soil are its main requirements.
PROPAGATION Sow the seeds directly where they are to grow in spring and early summer.
CULTIVARS 'Emperor Mixed' has a good range of flower colours.

Scabiosa atropurpurea (pin-cushion flower)
FLOWER COLOUR White, mauve, purple, pink and blue.
FLOWERING TIME Spring and early summer
DESCRIPTION Pretty flowers make this an attractive bedding plant.

CULTIVATION A hardy annual that prefers full sun and protection from strong winds. The soil should be well drained.
PROPAGATION Sow seed in punnets in autumn to early winter in temperate districts and autumn and spring in stems which reach a height of 50 cm.
CULTIVATION Grow in full sun or dappled shade. Viscaria will grow in light or heavy soil to which a mixed fertiliser has been added before planting.
PROPAGATION Sow seed directly where it is to grow in spring or early summer.
OTHER SPECIES *S. armeria* has grey-green, glaucous leaves and dark pink flowers.

Tagetes erecta (African marigold)
FLOWER COLOUR Lemon, yellow or deep orange
FLOWERING TIME Spring and summer
DESCRIPTION Grown for their strong-smelling, deep green foliage and colourful flowers.
CULTIVATION A sunny position and ample water during dry periods are the main requirements. Mulch around the plants with grass clippings or leaf mould during summer. Feed monthly with a soluble fertiliser but do not overfeed or the plants will run to foliage instead of bearing flowers.
PROPAGATION Sow seeds in punnets during spring. Sowing can continue until mid-summer for late summer and autumn flowering. Transplant to the garden when they are 5 cm high.
CULTIVARS There are many different varieties.
OTHER SPECIES *T. patula* (French marigold) has shades of red, yellow and orange. There are many different varieties of this species.

Torenia fournieri (wishbone flower)
FLOWER COLOUR Deep blue
FLOWERING TIME Summer
DESCRIPTION A free-flowering annual with blue snapdragon-like flowers. Suitable for low borders, edging and containers.
CULTIVATION Plant in full sun or partial shade in a well-drained but moist soil enriched with manure or compost.
PROPAGATION Sow the seeds in spring or early summer in punnets and transplant seedlings into the garden when they are 5 cm high.

CULTIVARS 'Little Gem' is the most popular variety.

Tropaeolum majus (nasturtium)
FLOWER COLOUR Orange, scarlet, red, mahogany, yellow or white.
FLOWERING TIME Spring, summer and autumn
DESCRIPTION Valued for their orbicular, bright green leaves and large, colourful flowers.
CULTIVATION Plant in moderately fertile soil otherwise lush growth is made at the expense of the flowers. Nasturtiums are tolerant of full sun or partial shade and prefer rather dry conditions.
PROPAGATION Sow seed directly where it is to grow from spring to late summer in temperate climates, and spring only in colder climates.
CULTIVARS 'Jewel Mixed' has compact plants. 'Cherry Rose' has double flowers. 'Whirly Bird' differs from other varieties as the flowers do not have a spur. 'Alaska' has marbled or variegated leaves. 'Roulette' produces a heavy crop of flowers.

Viola x wittrockiana (pansy)
FLOWER COLOUR Wide variety of colours
FLOWERING TIME Late winter, early spring and summer
DESCRIPTION Pansies are actually perennials but they are grown more widely as annuals. There are many flower forms. The velvety flowers may be veined, striped, blotched or edged with contrasting colours.
CULTIVATION Plant in full sun or dappled shade. Pansies like soil that has been enriched with organic matter. Picking the flowers regularly encourages more to appear.
PROPAGATION Seeds can be sown from early winter to mid-summer in most districts and autumn and spring in cold areas. Sow seeds in punnets and transplant to the garden when they are 5 cm high.
CULTIVARS *V. tricolor*, commonly called heartsease, bears masses of colourful purple and yellow, white-eyed flowers, like miniature pansies. *V. cornuta* has small, scented, violet-purple flowers.

Zinnia elegans (youth and old age)
FLOWER COLOUR Wide colour range
FLOWERING TIME Spring and summer
DESCRIPTION Popular flowering annuals which

BRIGHT YELLOW MARIGOLDS (*TAGETES* SPECIES)

are available in tall and dwarf varieties. The stiff, daisy-like flowers have a conspicuous centre of yellow stamens.
CULTIVATION A warm position and full sun with protection from wind are the main requirements of zinnias. Add organic matter and a complete fertiliser to the bed before planting.
PROPAGATION In temperate districts, sow the seed from early spring to early summer. In cold districts, late spring and early summer are best.
CULTIVARS 'Gold Medal' has large double blooms on strong stems. 'Showman' is a mixture resembling the dahlia-flowered types, having huge double flowers in a bright range of colours. 'Envy' has flowers in soft-lime to emerald green. 'Happy Talk' is valued for its large ruffled double flowers.
OTHER SPECIES *Z. haageana* has flowers in shades of yellow, orange and red.
CULTIVARS 'Persian Carpet' has flowers in shades of lemon, orange, lavender, crimson and maroon with white or gold markings on the tips of the petals.

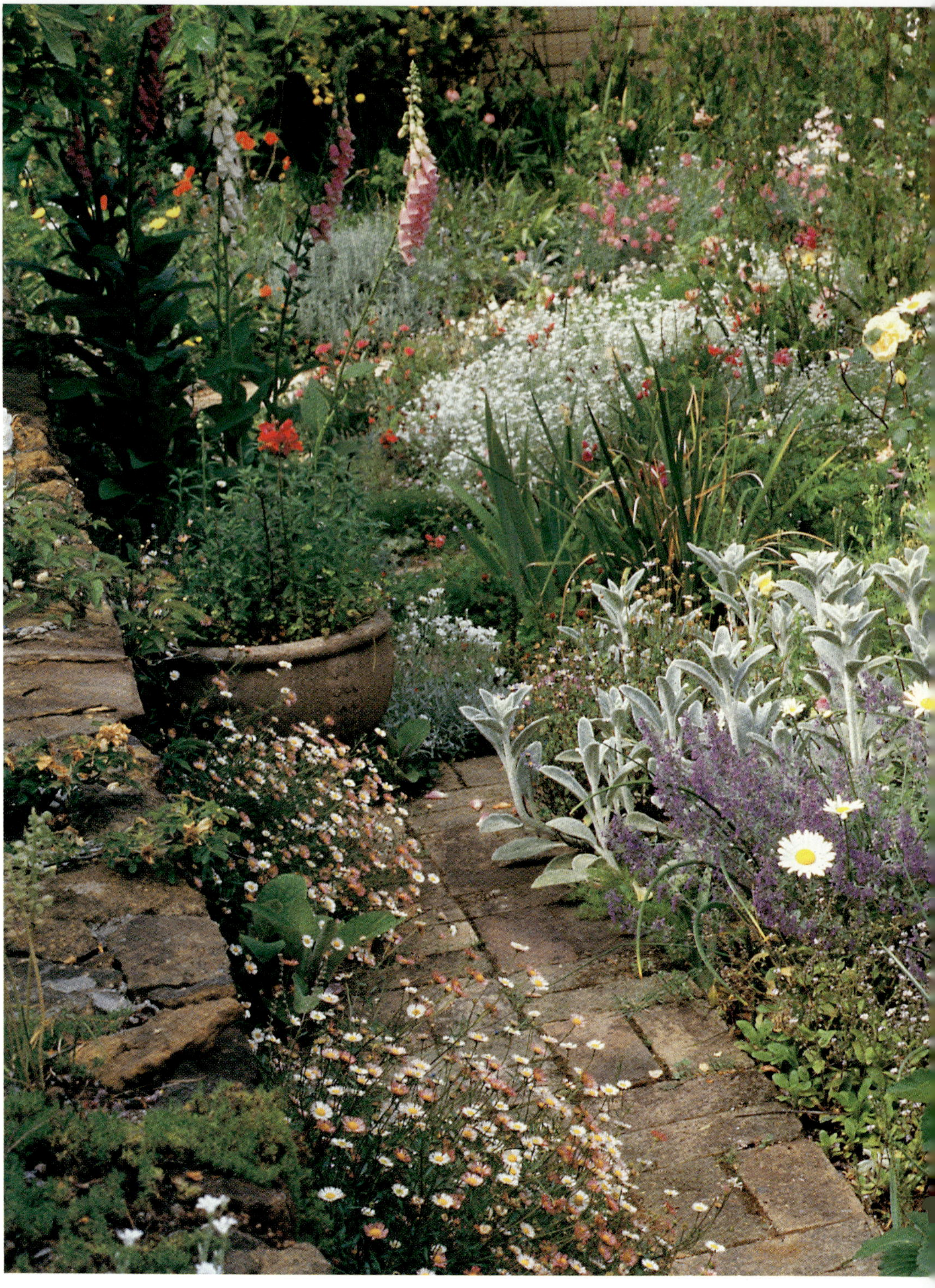

An informal collection of annuals and perennials

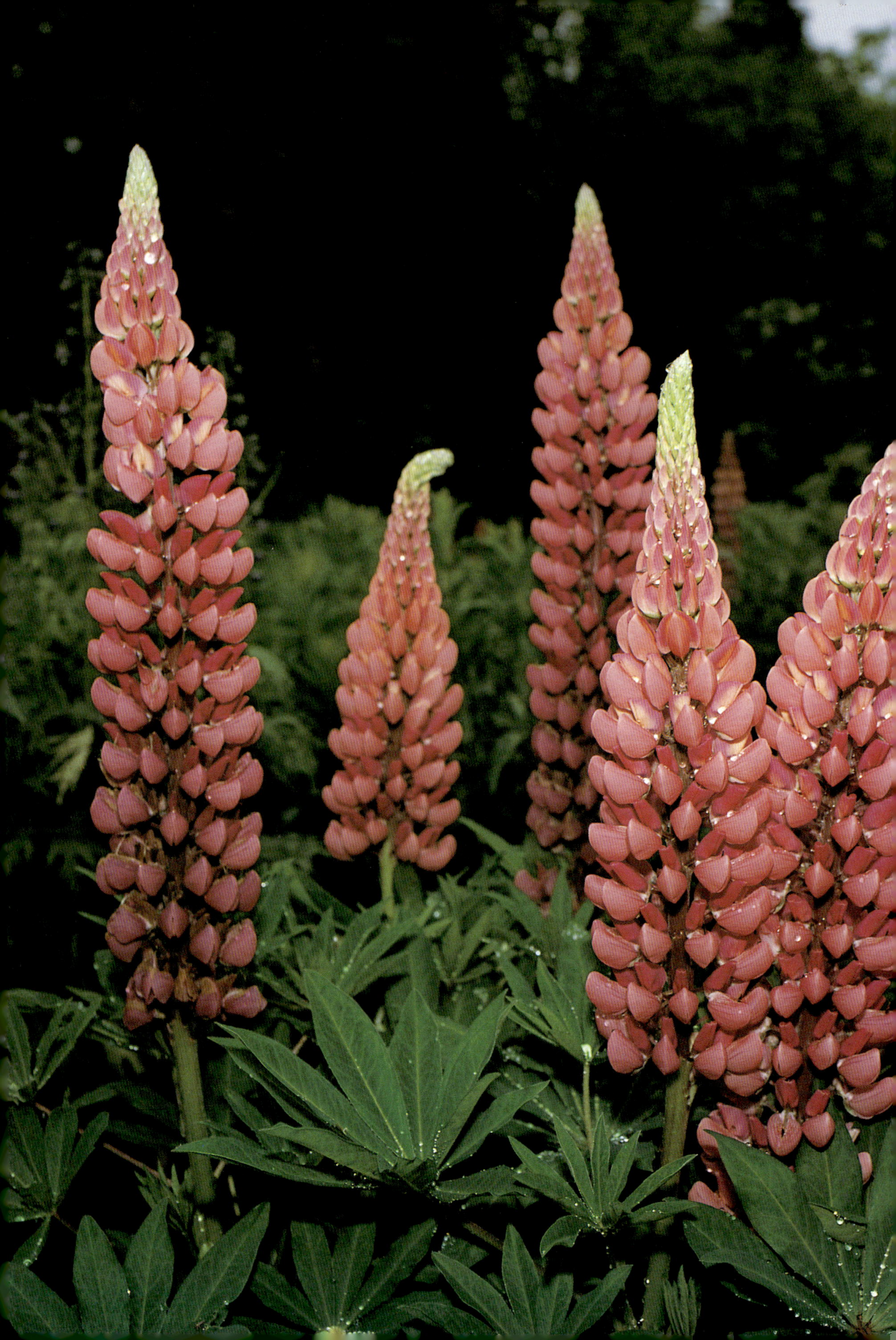

PERENNIALS
A Selection List

Acanthus mollis (oyster plant or bear's breeches)
FLOWER COLOUR Purple and white
FLOWERING TIME Summer
HEIGHT 1 m
DESCRIPTION Valued for its large, shiny, dark green leaves which radiate from a central point at ground level. The flowers are carried on tall spikes above the leaves.
CULTIVATION Oyster plant will thrive in sun or shade and in poor soil. But for best results mulch with manure or compost and keep watered during summer.
PROPAGATION Clumps may be lifted and divided during winter.
OTHER SPECIES *A. longifolius* has long, narrow, serrated leaves and spikes of large, rose-purple, lipped flowers. *A. montanus* reaches a height of 2 m. *A. spinosissimus* has handsome decorative foliage.

Achillea filipendulina (yarrow)
FLOWER COLOUR Bright yellow
FLOWERING TIME Summer
HEIGHT 75 cm–1 m
DESCRIPTION A pretty, herbaceous perennial with lacy green foliage and packed flowerheads consisting of tiny yellow blooms.
CULTIVATION A hardy plant that will give good results if planted in full sun and a well-drained soil. A mulch of organic matter during spring is beneficial.
PROPAGATION By division or seed in spring.
OTHER SPECIES *A. ageratum* is a slender herb with greenish grey leaves and yellow flowers. *A. grandiflora* reaches a height of 80 cm and has white flowers. *A. millefolium* has white flowers. *A. millefolium* 'Rosea' has pink flowers. *A. millefolium* 'Cerise Queen' bears crimson flowers. *A. ptarmica* has glossy green leaves and white flowers. *A. tomentosa* has a profusion of yellow flowers.

The magnificent flowerheads of lupins

Aconitum napellus (monkshood)
FLOWER COLOUR Deep blue
FLOWERING TIME Autumn
HEIGHT 60-80 cm
DESCRIPTION A hardy perennial having deeply-cut, dark green leaves and deep blue flowers.
CULTIVATION Grow monkshood in sun or semi-shade in any fertile, well-drained soil. Incoporate compost or manure into the soil prior to planting.
PROPAGATION Clumps may be lifted and divided during late winter or sow seed in spring.
OTHER SPECIES *A. fischeri* reaches a height of 1–2 m and bears violet-purple flowers.

Agastache mexicana (Mexican giant hyssop)
FLOWER COLOUR Crimson
FLOWERING TIME Summer
HEIGHT 75 cm
DESCRIPTION A clump-forming plant with serrated leaves and tall flower spikes.
CULTIVATION Grow in a sunny or lightly shaded position. Cut back to the basal clump after flowering.
PROPAGATION Seed or division in spring.
OTHER SPECIES *A. foeniculum* has tiny, mauve flowers on cylindrical spikes.

Ajuga reptans (bugle flower, carpet bugle)
FLOWER COLOUR Blue
FLOWERING TIME Summer
HEIGHT 10–20 cm
DESCRIPTION A marvellous, rapidly growing perennial that forms a good groundcover. The whorls of blue flowers sit above the dark green leaves.
CULTIVATION Bugle flower will thrive in full sun or shade and in poor soils. For best results plant in well-drained soil that has been enriched with organic matter.
PROPAGATION Divide clumps during winter.
CULTIVARS 'Burgundy Lace' has cream and maroon leaves. 'Multicolor' has reddish pink, burgundy and creamy yellow markings on the leaves. 'Alba' has white flowers. 'Jungle Beauty' has large green leaves and flower spikes.

Alcea rosea (hollyhock)
FLOWER COLOUR Various colours
FLOWERING TIME Summer

YARROW (*ACHILLEA MILLEFOLIUM*)

HEIGHT 2–3 m
DESCRIPTION Tall plants which look magnificent in cottage gardens. The flower spikes are packed with blooms.
CULTIVATION Hollyhocks prefer full sunlight and a position sheltered from strong winds. Stakes are generally required to keep them upright. Hollyhocks are adaptable to light and heavy soils. Protect from snails and slugs when they are young and when in flower.
PROPAGATION Sow seed in late summer or early autumn. Flowers generally appear the second year.
CULTIVARS 'Summer Carnival' is early flowering and reaches a height of 3 m. 'Double Mixed' is similar in size. 'Nigra' has blackish red flowers.

Alchemilla mollis (lady's mantle)
FLOWER COLOUR Yellow
FLOWERING TIME Spring
HEIGHT 35 cm
DESCRIPTION A clump-forming perennial that has rounded, pale green leaves.

ALSTROEMERIA AUREA

CULTIVATION Lady's mantle prefers a semi-shaded position. Apply a mulch in spring, water well in dry weather and trim back stems after flowering.
PROPAGATION Seed or divide clumps in spring.

Alonsoa warscewiczii (mask flower)
FLOWER COLOUR Varies from pink to red to orange
FLOWERING TIME Spring to autumn
HEIGHT 70 cm
DESCRIPTION A fleshy plant with slender stems and mid-green leaves.
CULTIVATION Mask flower prefers a warm climate. It will flower for months if given a moist but well-drained soil. Water thoroughly in dry weather.
PROPAGATION Cuttings or seed in spring.

Alstroemeria aurea (Peruvian lily, Chilean lily)
FLOWER COLOUR Orange, yellow, white, pink and red, depending on the hybrid
FLOWERING TIME Late spring and early summer
HEIGHT 60–90 cm
DESCRIPTION The orchid-like flowers are ideal for cutting. The plant forms a clumps and has fine leaves.
CULTIVATION Peruvian lily will grow in sun or semi-shade. Give ample water during summer and mulch in early spring with rich compost. An application of complete plant food when the buds form will encourage more flowers.
PROPAGATION Propagated from root divisions in early autumn.
OTHER SPECIES *A. pulchella* has red and green flowers.

Althea officinalis (marsh mallow)
FLOWER COLOUR Lilac-pink
FLOWERING TIME Summer and autumn
HEIGHT 1.5 m
DESCRIPTION A hardy perennial which has a hairy, erect stem and large leaves. Many mallows are considered to be weeds but some are also cultivated.
CULTIVATION Grow marsh mallow in full sun. It is tolerant of damp soil or saline conditions.
PROPAGATION Seed sown in spring.

Anchusa azurea (alkanet, Italian bugloss)
FLOWER COLOUR Blue
FLOWERING TIME Spring and summer
HEIGHT 1 m
DESCRIPTION The mid-green leaves are long and tapered. Once established in the garden it will readily self-seed.
CULTIVATION An easily-grown perennial which prefers a moist, lightly shaded situation. Plant under trees or among other tall-growing perennials.
PROPAGATION Seed sown in spring.
OTHER SPECIES *A. officinalis* has blue, violet or pink flowers. *A. capensis* is a biennial alkanet which will flower in the first summer if seeds are sown in autumn.

Anemone blanda (woodland anemone)
FLOWER COLOUR Blue, but pink, violet and white forms are available
FLOWERING TIME Spring
HEIGHT 15 cm
DESCRIPTION A pretty perennial that is ideal for naturalising underneath trees. The foliage is a soft green and the flowers are carried just above the leaves.

THE PRETTY PINK OR WHITE FLOWERS OF JAPANESE WINDFLOWER (*ANEMONE X HYBRIDA*)

CULTIVATION A shady, moist position will give good results with the woodland anemone. Add compost or manure to the soil before planting to help retain soil moisture.
PROPAGATION Once established in the garden it will freely self-seed.

Anemone x hybrida (Japanese windflower)
FLOWER COLOUR White, dark pink or mauve depending on the variety
FLOWERING TIME Late summer and autumn
HEIGHT 90 cm
DESCRIPTION Attractive, clump-forming plants which have tall flower stems carrying daisy-like blooms.
CULTIVATION For best results plant in a shaded position. Full sun will be tolerated but the roots must be kept mulched and cool. Keep moist during summer.
PROPAGATION Division of the root during winter or early spring.
OTHER SPECIES *A. coronaria* has red, blue-purple or white flowers in late winter or early spring. *A. rivularis* bears cymes of small, white nodding flowers in spring. *A. sylvestris* has fragrant, white flowers.

Aquilegia vulgaris (columbines, granny's bonnets)
FLOWER COLOUR Cream, pink, yellow, red or blue depending on the variety
FLOWERING TIME Spring
HEIGHT 75 cm
DESCRIPTION The funnel-shaped flowers carry a spur which gives the appearance of a granny's bonnet. The grey-green foliage has a fern-like appearance.
CULTIVATION Columbines like a well-drained soil enriched with organic matter. They will grow in sun or semi-shade. In cool climates plants will last for many years but in warmer climates it is best to start seedlings every second year.
PROPAGATION Sow seed in autumn in punnets and transplant when the seedlings are 5–7 cm tall. In cool climates the roots can be divided in winter. Once established in the garden columbines self-seed reliably.

OTHER SPECIES A. *alpina* is a dwarf columbine with deep blue flowers. *A. caerulea* is a parent of long-spurred hybrids. *A. flabellata* has white to violet-blue flowers. *A. x hybrida* has flowers of one colour or may be multicoloured.

Arabis caucasica (rock cress)
FLOWER COLOUR White
FLOWERING TIME Spring
HEIGHT 15–20 cm
DESCRIPTION The plants are loose and mat-forming with grey-green, hairy leaves clasping the stems. Suitable for rock gardens or for use between pavers.
CULTIVATION Rock cress is a hardy plant that will thrive in almost any soil type and full sun or partial shade.
PROPAGATION Root division during winter.
CULTIVARS 'Flore Pleno' has white flowers.

Arenaria montana (sandwort)
FLOWER COLOUR White
FLOWERING TIME Late spring
HEIGHT 15 cm
DESCRIPTION A pretty groundcover valued for its mid-green leaves and saucer-shaped flowers.
CULTIVATION For best results plant in a well-drained soil that has been enriched with compost or manure. Arenaria will grow in sun or partial shade.
PROPAGATION By seed or 3–5 cm basal shoot cuttings during summer.
OTHER SPECIES *A. balearica* reaches a height of only 6 cm and has white flowers.

Argemone hispida (prickly poppy)
FLOWER COLOUR White with yellow centres
FLOWERING TIME Summer and autumn
HEIGHT 1 m
DESCRIPTION A tender perennial which is usually grown as an annual. Looks similar to romneya.
CULTIVATION Grow in full sun in well-drained soil.
PROPAGATION Sow seed in spring when frosts have finished.

Armeria maritima (thrift or sea pink)
FLOWER COLOUR Pink
FLOWERING TIME Spring to summer
HEIGHT 10–12 cm
DESCRIPTION A useful edging or border plant with rich green, grass-like foliage. Erect and rigid stems bear individual flowerheads in the shape of a globe.
CULTIVATION Thrift prefers a light, open soil, full sun and will grow particularly well near the sea.
PROPAGATION Division or cuttings taken in early autumn or by seed.
OTHER SPECIES *A. pseudarmeria* 'Giant White' has white flowers. *A. pseudarmeria* 'Rubra' produces rosy red flowers.

Artemisia absinthium (wormwood)
FLOWER COLOUR Yellow
FLOWERING TIME Spring, summer and autumn
HEIGHT 1–1.2 m
DESCRIPTION Valued for its silvery-grey, much divided leaves. A good accent plant for a border.
CULTIVATION Wormwood likes a sunny position and well-drained soil.
PROPAGATION Tip cuttings taken in early spring.
OTHER SPECIES *A. frigida* is valued for its small button-shaped flowers and silver-grey foliage.

Artemisia lactiflora (Chinese mugwort)
FLOWER COLOUR Creamy-white
FLOWERING TIME Late summer to autumn
HEIGHT 120–150 cm
DESCRIPTION A useful plant for the back of the border. It has jagged, green leaves and conspicuous plumes of tiny long-lasting flowers.
CULTIVATION Chinese mugwort prefers full sun and a moist soil that has been enriched with manure or compost. Keep well watered during summer.
PROPAGATION Tip cuttings in spring.

Aster novi-belgii hybrids (Michaelmas daisy)
FLOWER COLOUR Mauve, pink, purple, lilac or white depending on the variety
FLOWERING TIME Mid-summer to autumn
HEIGHT 60–120 cm
DESCRIPTION A delightful, bushy perennial which has daisy-like flowers massed along tall flower spikes. Can be quite invasive.
CULTIVATION For good results plant in a sunny

GOAT'S BEARD (*ASTILBE X ARENDSII*)

position. The soil should be rich in organic matter and well-drained.
PROPAGATION By division in later autumn or immediately after flowering.
OTHER SPECIES *A. alpinus* bears white, purple or pink, yellow-centred daisy flowers in summer. *A. amellus* has large pink or lilac-blue flowers in summer and autumn. *A. x frikartii* is a hybrid with large violet-blue flowers and a golden centre. *A. laevis* has pale violet-blue flowers.

Astilbe x arendsii (goat's beard)
FLOWER COLOUR White and shades of pink or red depending on the variety
FLOWERING TIME Spring
HEIGHT 90 cm
DESCRIPTION Astilbes look most effective when planted on the edges of pools or beside streams. The plumed heads of feathery flowers are carried above the shining fern-like foliage.
CULTIVATION Astilbes prefer a shady position but will tolerate some sun if the soil is kept moist. They thrive in a moist but well-drained soil enriched with generous amounts of organic matter. A mulch of cow manure or compost in late winter before the new spring growth is most beneficial.
PROPAGATION Root divisions in winter.
OTHER SPECIES *A. chinensis* is a dwarf astilbe.

Astrantia major (masterwort)
FLOWER COLOUR The pinkish green flowers are surrounded by a frill of papery bracts.
FLOWERING TIME Spring
HEIGHT 60 cm
DESCRIPTION An unusual plant having leaves comprised of three to seven ovate leaflets.
CULTIVATION A shade-loving perennial which prefers a moisture-retentive soil and ample summer water.
PROPAGATION Propagate by seed or division in spring.
CULTIVARS 'Shaggy' has larger bracts.
OTHER SPECIES *A. maxima* reaches a height of 80 cm and has rose-pink bracts.

Aubrieta deltoidea (rock cress)
FLOWER COLOUR Rose-lilac to purple or blue
FLOWERING TIME Spring and summer
HEIGHT 10 cm
DESCRIPTION A pretty perennial groundcover that forms a dense mat of colour. The foliage is grey-green.
CULTIVATION Rock cress prefers a sunny position and an alkaline soil. It will tolerate dry conditions. After flowering cut the plants back quite hard to encourage new growth.
PROPAGATION Divide established plants in autumn.

Aurinia saxatilis syn. *Alyssum saxatile* (yellow alyssum)
FLOWER COLOUR Yellow
FLOWERING TIME Spring to early summer
HEIGHT 25–30 cm
DESCRIPTION An evergreen perennial with grey-green leaves. Excellent for walls or rock gardens.
CULTIVATION Yellow alyssum will grow in any well-drained garden soil and a sunny position.
PROPAGATION Easily raised from seed or by 5–8 cm long cuttings taken in early summer.

Bellis perennis (lawn or English daisy)
FLOWER COLOUR White tinged with pink and

yellow centres
FLOWERING TIME Spring
HEIGHT 10 cm
DESCRIPTION Dainty plants with shiny, deep green foliage and small daisy-like flowers. The older varieties look pretty when grown in lawns.
CULTIVATION Lawn daisies will grow in sun or semi-shade in any well-drained soil. They will readily self-seed once established in the garden.
PROPAGATION Seed may be sown in autumn but in cold climates it can also be sown in spring.

Bergenia x schmidtii (Norwegian snow, heartleaf bergenia)
FLOWER COLOUR Rose-pink or white
FLOWERING TIME Late winter to early spring
HEIGHT 35 cm
DESCRIPTION A hardy evergreen perennial with large, fleshy, heart-shaped leaves. The flowers are borne on short stalks.
CULTIVATION A very adaptable plant that will grow in sun or full shade. It is tolerant of poor soils but looks its best when planted in a soil that has been enriched with organic matter.
PROPAGATION Plant division in spring.

Brachycome multifida (Swan River daisy)
FLOWER COLOUR Lilac-blue
FLOWERING TIME Spring and summer
HEIGHT 10–30 cm
DESCRIPTION Grown for its profusion of daisy-like flowers and its tidy habit. Grow Swan River daisy in the rock garden or let it trail over a wall or the side of a large pot.
CULTIVATION A position in full sun or dappled shade and a well-drained soil are its main requirements.
PROPAGATION Seed
OTHER SPECIES *B. angustifolia* is a mat-forming groundcover.

Brunnera macrophylla (summer forget-me-not, Siberian bugloss)
FLOWER COLOUR Blue
FLOWERING TIME Summer
HEIGHT 45 cm
DESCRIPTION Grown for its forget-me-not-like flowers and heart-shaped foliage. Plant *en masse* in the border.
CULTIVATION A hardy plant that will perform well in even the poorest soil.
PROPAGATION Root division in winter or seed sown directly where it is to grow.

Campanula isophylla (Italian bellflower)
FLOWER COLOUR Pale blue
FLOWERING TIME Late spring to summer
HEIGHT 30–45 cm
DESCRIPTION Valued for its star-shaped flowers and heart-shaped foliage.
CULTIVATION For best results plant in a well-drained soil that has been enriched with compost or manure. Italian bellflower will grow in full sun or partial shade.
PROPAGATION Root divisions in late winter or cuttings in spring.
CULTIVARS *C. isophylla* 'Alba' has white flowers.

Campanula persicifolia (peach-leaved campanula)
FLOWER COLOUR Blue or white depending on the variety
FLOWERING TIME Late spring to mid-summer
HEIGHT 90 cm
DESCRIPTION The bell-shaped flowers are 2.5 cm across.
CULTIVATION Plant in a well-drained soil that has been enriched with organic matter. Grows well in light shade.
PROPAGATION Spring-sown seeds or division.

Campanula portenschlagiana (Dalmatian bellflower)
FLOWER COLOUR Blue
FLOWERING TIME Spring to early summer
HEIGHT 15 cm
DESCRIPTION Large, bell-shaped flowers cover the heart-shaped foliage. A good rock garden or border plant.
CULTIVATION A well-drained soil and a sunny position will give good results.
PROPAGATION By cuttings or root division during spring.

Campanula rotundifolia (English harebell or blue bells of Scotland)
FLOWER COLOUR Violet-blue

FLOWERING TIME Mid-spring to late summer
HEIGHT 25–50 cm
DESCRIPTION Valued for its 1.75 cm long, bell-shaped flowers and heart-shaped foliage. An ideal rock garden, groundcover or basket plant.
CULTIVATION A sunny position and a soil that is rich in organic matter will give good results.
PROPAGATION Cuttings or root division during spring.
CULTIVARS *C. rotundifolia* 'Alba' has white flowers.
OTHER SPECIES *C. barbata* has white summer flowers. *C. carpatica* produces blue flowers. *C. glomerata* has purple-blue flowers. *C. latifolia* reaches a height of 1.5 m and has purple-blue flowers. *C. pyramidalis* has white or blue flowers.

Catananche caerulea (cupid's dart)
FLOWER COLOUR Blue
FLOWERING TIME Summer and autumn
HEIGHT 50 cm
DESCRIPTION Cupid's dart forms a rosette of grey-green leaves. The wiry stems bear solitary, silver buds which open to blue flowers. A pretty plant for the front of the border.
CULTIVATION This is the perfect plant for a sunny, dry garden. Cupid's dart prefers a temperate climate.
PROPAGATION Seed sown in spring.

Centaurea dealbata (Persian knapweed, pink cornflower)
FLOWER COLOUR Pink
FLOWERING TIME Summer and autumn
HEIGHT 60 cm
DESCRIPTION An attractive perennial which spreads by underground stems. The large, pinnate leaves have a silver underside. The flowers have a thistle-like appearance.
CULTIVATION Persian knapweed prefers a sunny position and well-drained soil. It is tolerant of dry conditions. The stems may be cut back after flowering.
PROPAGATION By seed or basal cutting.
OTHER SPECIES *C. gymnocarpa* is a shrubby perennial with silver leaves and small violet flowers. *C. montana* has silvery-green leaves and large blue-violet flowers.

Centranthus ruber (red valerian)
FLOWER COLOUR Pale rose-red
FLOWERING TIME Spring to late summer
HEIGHT 45–90 cm
DESCRIPTION Grown for its profusion of flowers and bluish green foliage. Plant in the herbaceous border or between shrubs.
CULTIVATION Suited to light shade or full sun. Red valerian will thrive in any well-drained garden soil. Prune spent flower stems and keep moist during dry periods.
PROPAGATION Seeds sown in autumn, root divisions in winter or cuttings in summer.
CULTIVARS *C. ruber* 'Albus' has white flowers.

Cerastium tomentosum (snow in summer)
FLOWER COLOUR White
FLOWERING TIME Spring to summer
HEIGHT 10–15 cm
DESCRIPTION A low, evergreen perennial valued for its silvery-white foliage. Use as groundcover or let it tumble over a wall.
CULTIVATION A hardy plant that will grow in any well-drained soil and a position in full sun. Clip off the spent flowerheads.
PROPAGATION Division during winter.

Chrysanthemum cinerariifolium (true pyrethrum)
FLOWER COLOUR White with yellow centres
FLOWERING TIME Spring
HEIGHT 70 cm
DESCRIPTION This perennial herb has fern-like foliage. Commercially, this herb is used to make a non-toxic insecticide.
CULTIVATION A pretty plant for a cottage garden. Plant in full sun and well-drained soil. Dead-head spent blooms and cut back stems to the basal clump after flowering.
PROPAGATION Seed sown in autumn or spring.

Chrysanthemum coccineum syn. *Pyrethrum roseum* (red pyrethrum)
FLOWER COLOUR Shades of rose, lilac, scarlet and carmine
FLOWERING TIME Summer
HEIGHT 30–60 cm
DESCRIPTION A pretty perennial for the garden border. The flowers may be single and daisy-like or double and pincushion-like. The dark green foliage has a strong smell.
CULTIVATION Plant in full sun and a well-drained soil.
PROPAGATION Division of the clump in early spring.

MARGUERITE DAISY (*CHRYSANTHEMUM FRUTESCANS*)

Chrysanthemum frutescans (Marguerite daisy)
FLOWER COLOUR White, pink or yellow
FLOWERING TIME Late winter to autumn
HEIGHT 90 cm
DESCRIPTION A fast-growing shrubby perennial valued for its ease of growth, free-flowering habit and dainty foliage.
CULTIVATION Marguerite daisy will grow in any soil type and a position in full sun. Prune back hard after flowering.
PROPAGATION Cuttings taken during late winter and early spring.
CULTIVARS There are numerous named varieties with double and single flowers.

Chrysanthemum morifolium (perennial chrysanthemum)
FLOWER COLOUR White, cream and shades of mauve, pink, burgundy and yellow
FLOWERING TIME Autumn
HEIGHT 60cm–1 m
DESCRIPTION Valuable plants for the perennial border. There are numerous flower types with single, semi-double and double flowers. Some types have quilled petals.
CULTIVATION Plant in a warm, sunny position in a heavy or light soil.
PROPAGATION Seed sown in spring or division of the old clump in early spring.

Chrysanthemum parthenium syn. ***Matricaria eximia*** (feverfew)
FLOWER COLOUR White with a yellow centre
FLOWERING TIME Late spring to late summer
HEIGHT 60 cm
DESCRIPTION The strong-scented leaves are deeply serrated. Use in clumps in the border.
CULTIVATION A sunny position and a well-drained soil will give good results. Add manure or compost to the soil before planting.
PROPAGATION Seed sown in spring.
CULTIVARS 'Aureum' has golden foliage and insignificant flowers.

Chrysanthemum superbum
syn. *C. maximum* (shasta daisy)
FLOWER COLOUR White with yellow centres
FLOWERING TIME Late spring to late summer
HEIGHT 60–90 cm
DESCRIPTION The tall flower stems arise from the dense mat of foliage which does not die down completely in warm climates. The large daisy-like flowers have a conspicuous golden centre.
CULTIVATION A hardy plant that will grow in any soil type and a sunny position. Picking the flowers as they finish will encourage repeat flowering.
PROPAGATION Division of the root in early spring.

Cynara cardunculus (cardoon)
FLOWER COLOUR Purple
FLOWERING TIME Summer
HEIGHT 2 m
DESCRIPTION A spectacular perennial which has spiny, grey-green leaves with a woolly underside. The stems are eaten as a vegetable.
CULTIVATION Grow at the back of the border in full sun and well-drained soil. Pick the flowers regularly and divide suckers off the main plant for replanting every few years.
PROPAGATION Seed sown in spring.

Dahlia hybrids (bedding dahlias)
FLOWER COLOUR White and shades of red, yellow and orange
FLOWERING TIME Early summer to autumn
HEIGHT 30–70 cm high
DESCRIPTION Very free-flowering plants having semi-double and double flowers.
CULTIVATION Plant in full sun or light shade in a fertile, well-drained soil.
PROPAGATION Sow seed in spring or early summer.

Dahlia imperialis (tree dahlia)
FLOWER COLOUR Lilac-pink
FLOWERING TIME Autumn
HEIGHT 1.5–2m
DESCRIPTION A tall perennial suitable for background planting. The long bipinnate leaves usually fall from the lower stems, leaving the branches bared.
CULTIVATION For best results the tree dahlia requires protection from strong winds and a rich, friable soil. Cut out the non-productive stems in early spring.
PROPAGATION Take 60 cm cuttings after flowering.

Delphinium elatum 'Pacific Giant'
FLOWER COLOUR Pink, white, lavender, violet or blue
FLOWERING TIME Late spring to early summer
HEIGHT 1–2 m
DESCRIPTION Stately flowers on tall stems make these hybrids most striking when grown in a cottage garden border. Although they are perennials, they are generally treated as annuals.
CULTIVATION Grow in moist soil in full sun and stake them if they are in a windy position. They are very susceptible to snails and slugs.
PROPAGATION Seed or, in cool climates, division of the roots immediately after flowering or as soon as new growth begins in spring.
CULTIVARS 'Mighty Atom and 'Blue Tit' are dwarf varieties.

Dianthus x allwoodii (allwood pink)
FLOWER COLOUR Pink, white or red or combinations of these
FLOWERING TIME Spring to summer
HEIGHT 45 cm
DESCRIPTION A hybrid whose flowers are fringed or plain-petalled and can be single, double or semi-double. The foliage is grey-green.
CULTIVATION Allwood pink is easy to grow in any garden soil but requires good drainage and an alkaline soil. Manure or compost should be added to the soil before planting. Removing the spent flowers will prolong the flowering period.
PROPAGATION Spring cuttings.

Dianthus caryophyllus (carnation)
FLOWER COLOUR Red, pink, mauve, purple, burgundy, white and yellow
FLOWERING TIME Spring and autumn but often in flower at other times throughout the year
HEIGHT 30–40 cm
DESCRIPTION Evergreen perennials with grey-green foliage and 5–10 cm flowers which are carried on 40–60 cm long stems.

Delphiniums

CULTIVATION Plant in a sunny position and a rich, friable, well-drained soil. Remove dead flowers and cut back hard after flowering has finished.
PROPAGATION Sow seed in autumn or spring.
CULTIVARS There are many different varieties.

Dianthus deltoides (maiden pink, pink)
FLOWER COLOUR Pink
FLOWERING TIME Summer
HEIGHT 10 cm
DESCRIPTION The pretty, 5-petalled flowers sit 10 cm above the grey, grass-like foliage. Makes an enchanting edging plant.
CULTIVATION For best results plant in a rich, well-drained soil and a sunny position. Old growth can be removed from the clump during winter.
PROPAGATION Seed sown in autumn or spring or divide the clump in early spring.

Dianthus plumarius (garden or cottage pink)
FLOWER COLOUR Shades of red, pink, purple-red, mauve or white depending on the variety
FLOWERING TIME Spring
HEIGHT 20–30 cm
DESCRIPTION The fragant flowers sit above the 20 cm high grass-like leaves. Use as edging or rock garden plants.
CULTIVATION An open, sunny position and an alkaline well-drained soil are the main requirements for success with this plant.
PROPAGATION Seed or division of the clump in spring.
CULTIVARS There are many different varieties. Some have a coloured 'eye' while others have fringed petals. Among the most popular are 'Mrs. Sinkins', which has double white flowers, and 'Old English', which has double mauve-pink flowers.

Dicentra spectabilis (bleeding heart)
FLOWER COLOUR Deep pink and white
FLOWERING TIME Spring
HEIGHT 60 cm
DESCRIPTION The elegant, heart-shaped flowers droop from arching, horizontal stems. The foliage has a delicate fern-like appearance. Use near water or in clumps through the garden.
CULTIVATION Bleeding heart should be planted in a shady position in a rich, free-draining but moisture-retentive soil. It dies back in late summer to reappear in spring.
PROPAGATION Division of the roots in winter or early spring as the new growth appears.
CULTIVARS *Dicentra spectabilis* 'Alba' has white flowers.
OTHER SPECIES *D. formosa* has pink to crimson flowers in spring.

Dictamnus albus (burning bush)
FLOWER COLOUR White
FLOWERING TIME Summer
HEIGHT 60 cm
DESCRIPTION A bushy perennial which is worth growing for the tangy lemon perfume of its leaves and for its elegant flowers.
CULTIVATION Plant in a sunny position and a well-drained soil that has been enriched with organic matter.
PROPAGATION By seed.

Dierama pulcherrimum (fairy fishing rod)
FLOWER COLOUR pink
FLOWERING TIME Late spring and early summer
HEIGHT 1 m
DESCRIPTION A tussocky plant with grass-like leaves and arching stems which bear pendant, bell-shaped flowers.
CULTIVATION Fairy fishing rod will tolerate hot sun and can survive damp or dry conditions.
PROPAGATION By seed or divide corms in spring.

Digitalis ferruginea (rusty foxglove)
FLOWER COLOUR Pale yellow
FLOWERING TIME 1.5 m
HEIGHT 1.5 m
DESCRIPTION A short-lived perennial with a clump of narrow, tapered leaves from which the tall flower stem arises. The yellow tubular flowers are veined with a rusty red.
CULTIVATION Grow in full sun or partial shade in a moist but well-drained soil.
PROPAGATION Seed sown in autumn.
OTHER SPECIES *D. grandiflora* has soft, yellow flowers with brown markings inside. *D.* x *heywoodii* has felted white leaves and lemon tubular flowers. *D. lanata* has white, hairy leaves and whitish yellow flowers. *D. lutea* has yellow flowers. *D.* x *mertonensis* has

FOXGLOVES (*DIGITALIS PURPUREA*)

flowers the colour of crushed strawberries. *D. viridiflora* bears lime green, tubular flowers.

Digitalis purpurea (foxglove)
FLOWER COLOUR Purple, red, maroon, cream or pink
FLOWERING TIME Summer
HEIGHT 1–1.5 m
DESCRIPTION A biennial plant grown for its tall spires of spring and summer bell-shaped flowers which arise from a rosette of grey-green foliage. Foxgloves make spectacular cottage garden plants.
CULTIVATION A lightly shaded or sunny position will give good results with foxgloves. The soil should be enriched with organic matter prior to planting. Once planted in the garden they will freely self-seed.
PROPAGATION Sow the seed directly where it is to grow.

Doronicum plantagineum (leopard's bane)
FLOWER COLOUR Yellow
FLOWERING TIME Spring
HEIGHT 20–25 cm
DESCRIPTION Grown for its green heart-shaped foliage, yellow daisy-like flowers and its rapid growth.
CULTIVATION Leopard's bane requires a partially shaded position and an acidic, well-drained soil that has been enriched with copious amounts of organic matter.
PROPAGATION Root division during winter.

Echinacea purpurea (purple coneflower)
FLOWER COLOUR Reddish-purple, but there are also white, pink and yellow-flowering varieties
FLOWERING TIME Summer and autumn
HEIGHT 1.5 m
DESCRIPTION A pretty perennial with broad, ovate leaves. The large flowerheads have conical centres and sparse, drooping, outer florettes.
CULTIVATION Plant coneflower in full sun in any well-drained soil. Mulch with manure in spring and dead-head faded blooms.
PROPAGATION Seed or division in spring.

Echinops ritro (globe thistle)
FLOWER COLOUR Metallic blue-white
FLOWERING TIME Summer
HEIGHT 90–120 cm
DESCRIPTION A bold, old-fashioned, thistle-like plant which is useful for an herbaceous border. The blue flowers and the whitish grey foliage look most attractive when used in dried floral arrangements.
CULTIVATION Grow in full sun and any well-drained garden soil. Apply a handful of mixed fertiliser in early spring. May be cut back after flowering
PROPAGATION By division or seed.
CULTIVARS 'Veitch's Blue' is grown for its handsome flowerheads.
OTHER SPECIES E. bannaticus has grey-blue flowers in summer.

Echium fastuosum (bee plant, viper's bugloss)
FLOWER COLOUR Lilac-purple
FLOWERING TIME Mid-spring to mid-summer
HEIGHT 150 cm
DESCRIPTION A woody perennial which has a shrub-like appearance. The 30 cm long flower spikes are tightly packed with long-stamened, purplish blue flowers. Viper's bugloss is an ideal plant for growing near the sea.
CULTIVATION For best results plant in well-drained soil and full sun. It tends to flower more profusely in poor and dry soils. Cut off the older rosettes after flowering.
PROPAGATION Seed or short side shoots cut from the main stem as cuttings.
OTHER SPECIES E. candicans is similar to the above except for narrower leaves and pale blue or whitish flowers.

Erigeron karvinskianus (babies' tears)
FLOWER COLOUR Pink and white
FLOWERING TIME Spring to autumn
HEIGHT 15–25 cm
DESCRIPTION Grown for it profusion of white daisy-like flowers which become rose-pink with age.
CULTIVATION A hardy plant that will grow in full sun or light shade. Mulch around the plant in spring with manure or compost. Trim in late autumn after flowering has finished.
PROPAGATION Seed sown during winter. Erigeron self-seeds so prolifically that there are always new plants in the garden.

Eryngium maritimum (sea holly)
FLOWER COLOUR Violet-blue
FLOWERING TIME Summer
HEIGHT 40 cm
DESCRIPTION An interesting plant with a thistle-like appearance. It has stiff, spiny, lobed, greyish leaves and rounded flowerheads. The flowers dry well for indoor decoration.
CULTIVATION Sea holly will tolerate poor soils and dry conditions. Plant in a sunny position and well-drained soil.
PROPAGATION Seed sown in autumn.

Euphorbia amygdaloides (wood spurge)
FLOWER COLOUR Yellow-green bracts
FLOWERING TIME Spring and summer

THE PRETTY YELLOW FLOWERS OF EUPHORBIA APPEAR IN EARLY SPRING

HEIGHT 75 cm
DESCRIPTION An evergreen perennial with whorls of narrow, green leaves. The yellowish 'flowers' are actually bracts which surround the small flower.
CULTIVATION An extremely hardy perennial which is drought-tolerant. Wood spurge will thrive in a sunny position but will tolerate light shade.
PROPAGATION Seed or division.
CULTIVARS 'Purpurea' has reddish purple bracts and is tolerant of moist soil and shade.
OTHER SPECIES *E. characias* reaches a height of 1.5 m and has greyish leaves. The variety 'Wulfenii' is more robust and has brighter yellow bracts. *E. epithymoides* has red autumn leaves. *E. robbiae* grows well in the shade but needs room to spread.

Felicia amelloides (blue marguerite, blue daisy)
FLOWER COLOUR Blue with a yellow centre
FLOWERING TIME All seasons
HEIGHT 50 cm
DESCRIPTION An extremely free-flowering, evergreen perennial which has aromatic foliage and a broad spreading habit. An ideal rock garden or border plant.
CULTIVATION Plant in an open, sunny position and well-drained, rich soil. Prune back hard in late winter.
PROPAGATION Take cuttings in summer.

Filipendula purpurea (lace plant, meadowsweet)
FLOWER COLOUR Purple
FLOWERING TIME Summer

HEIGHT 1.2 m
DESCRIPTION An attractive perennial having fern-like foliage. Use as a background plant in the herbaceous border or plant between shrubs.
CULTIVATION For best results plant in semi-shade and a moist soil that has been enriched with copious amounts of organic matter. Cut back after flowering.
PROPAGATION Root division or seed sown in spring.
OTHER SPECIES *F. ulmaria* has reddish stems and small, cream flowers.

Gazania x hybrida (gazania)
FLOWER COLOUR White, cream, yellow, red or brown
FLOWERING TIME Spring and summer
HEIGHT 25 cm
DESCRIPTION A hardy evergreen perennial which is excellent when used as a groundcover or rock garden plant.
CULTIVATION An easily grown perennial which prefers very well-drained sandy soil and full sun. To prevent fungal attack do not over-fertilise and avoid over-watering.
PROPAGATION Division of the clump in late winter or early spring.
CULTIVARS 'Sunshine' has large flowers in a wide colour range. There are many different varieties, including two-tone varieties and black-centred varieties.

Gentiana acaulis (gentian)
FLOWER COLOUR Deep blue
FLOWERING TIME Spring
HEIGHT 10 cm
DESCRIPTION A delightful perennial that grows wild in the alpine meadows of Europe. It produces a glorious carpet of vivid blue flowers that enhance garden edges and rock garden pockets. May be planted in drifts as a groundcover.
CULTIVATION Gentian requires cool, moist, light, well-drained soil. If it produces leaves but no flowers, it needs to be moved to a warmer position. Plant in a sun or semi-shade.
PROPAGATION By division in late winter or seed sown in autumn.
OTHER SPECIES *G. lutea* has yellow flowers during summer.

Geranium endressii (pink crane's bill)
FLOWER COLOUR Pink
FLOWERING TIME Spring to autumn
HEIGHT 30 cm
DESCRIPTION A sprawling evergreen perennial with lobed leaves. A very pretty groundcover.
CULTIVATION Plant in a sheltered, lightly shaded position in moist but well-drained soil. In cold climates it will tolerate full sun. Water well during dry weather.
PROPAGATION Seed or a cutting from the basal clump.
CULTIVARS 'Wargrave Pink' has salmon pink flowers.

Geranium himalayense (crane's bill)
FLOWER COLOUR Violet-blue
FLOWERING TIME Spring and summer
HEIGHT 30 cm
DESCRIPTION A spreading perennial with large green leaves.
CULTIVATION Plant in a sheltered, lightly shaded position in moist but well-drained soil. Crane's bill may be cut back after flowering if it becomes straggly.
PROPAGATION Seed or a cutting from the basal clump.

Geranium ibericum (Iberian crane's bill)
FLOWER COLOUR Violet
FLOWERING TIME Summer
HEIGHT 45 cm
DESCRIPTION Valued for its deeply lobed and toothed leaves and colourful flowers. Makes an interesting groundcover.
CULTIVATION Grow in full sun or semi-shade. The soil should be free-draining and enriched with manure.
PROPAGATION By division during winter or from seed sown in summer or autumn.
CULTIVARS There is a white-flowering variety.

Geranium pratense (meadow crane's bill)
FLOWER COLOUR Blue
FLOWERING TIME Summer
HEIGHT 75 cm
DESCRIPTION The deeply cut leaves make this a most attractive plant. Use as a groundcover or for colour in the border.
CULTIVATION Suitable for full sun or semi-shade.
PROPAGATION Division during winter or by seed sown in summer or autumn.

CULTIVARS *G. pratense* 'Alba' has white flowers.

Geranium sanguineum (bloody crane's bill)
FLOWER COLOUR Magenta
FLOWERING TIME Late spring and summer
HEIGHT 45 cm
DESCRIPTION Valued for its deeply lobed leaves and profusion of flowers. Use as a groundcover, to trail over walls and in the rock garden.
CULTIVATION For best results plant in full sun and a well-drained, fertile soil.
PROPAGATION Division during winter or by seed sown in summer or autumn.
CULTIVARS 'Album' has white flowers.

Geum quellyon (scarlet avens)
FLOWER COLOUR Scarlet
FLOWERING TIME Late spring to early autumn
HEIGHT 45–50 cm
DESCRIPTION A charming old-fashioned perennial with coarsely toothed, hairy leaves and flowers carried on tall stems. Grow in the herbaceous border.
CULTIVATION Grow in moderately rich soil with good drainage. Full sun or light shade is acceptable.
PROPAGATION Division or seed in early spring.
CULTIVARS There are many different varieties having flower colours of orange, red or yellow.

Gypsophila paniculata (baby's breath)
FLOWER COLOUR White
FLOWERING TIME Summer
HEIGHT 90 cm
DESCRIPTION The fairy-like clusters of tiny flowers are carried above the light grey-green foliage.
CULTIVATION A position in full sun or semi shade and a rich friable soil will give good results.
PROPAGATION Root division during winter or seed sown in autumn.
CULTIVARS 'Bristol Fairy' has double white flowers. 'Flamingo' has double pink flowers. 'Rosy veil' has double pink flowers.

Gypsophila repens (fairy grass)
FLOWER COLOUR Pink or white
FLOWERING TIME Spring and summer
HEIGHT 20 cm
DESCRIPTION A pretty trailing perennial which is invaluable for the rock garden or between paving.
CULTIVATION Plant in full sun or light shade in a rich but well-drained soil.
PROPAGATION Seed sown in autumn or root division in winter.
CULTIVARS 'Rosea' bears a profusion of pale pink flowers.

Hedychium flavum (ginger lily)
FLOWER COLOUR Yellow with long red filaments
FLOWERING TIME Summer to autumn
HEIGHT 1–1.5 m
DESCRIPTION The tall stems have large leaves for most of their length and are topped with a large flowerhead composed of many orchid-like flowers which produce a spicy fragrance.
CULTIVATION Ginger lily requires a moist soil enriched with manure or compost and a position in full sun or shade. The flowering stems should be cut back to ground level during winter.
PROPAGATION Division of the rhizome during winter.

Helenium autumnale (sneeze weed)
FLOWER COLOUR Yellow
FLOWERING TIME Summer to early autumn
HEIGHT 120–150 cm
DESCRIPTION A beautiful perennial that is usually completely smothered in flowers. It makes a good background plant or can be planted *en masse* in a large area.
CULTIVATION Sneeze weed will grow in almost any well-drained soil. Requires full sun.
PROPAGATION Division in autumn or spring.

Helianthemum nummularium (sun rose)
FLOWER COLOUR Yellow
FLOWERING TIME Mid-spring to mid-summer
HEIGHT 25–30 cm
DESCRIPTION An evergreen perennial valued for its dark green foliage which is paler on the underside. The 2.5 cm flowers are saucer-shaped.
CULTIVATION Plant in full sun in any well-drained, average soil and fertilise in spring with a complete plant food. Pinching out the growing tips will keep the plant bushy.
PROPAGATION Cuttings taken in summer
CULTIVARS There are many named varieties.

Helichrysum bracteatum (strawflower)
FLOWER COLOUR Yellow, orange, pink or white bracts depending on the variety
FLOWERING TIME Summer
HEIGHT 1 m
DESCRIPTION An Australian native which has tapered, green leaves and wiry stems topped with colourful flowers.
CULTIVATION Extremely hardy, sun-loving plants which thrive in a dry, free-draining soil. The cut flowers are everlasting.
PROPAGATION By seed, cutting or division.
CULTIVARS 'Monstrosum' has large flowers. 'Namum' is a dwarf variety.
OTHER SPECIES *H. angustifolium* has silver leaves and tiny, golden flowers during summer.

Helleborus foetidus (stinking hellebore)
FLOWER COLOUR Pale green, edged with maroon
FLOWERING TIME Winter and early spring
HEIGHT 80 cm
DESCRIPTION The bell-shaped flowers sit above the deep green, segmented leaves.
CULTIVATION Stinking hellebore prefers a moist soil and light shade.
PROPAGATION By division in autumn or seed sown in spring.

Helleborus lividus (Corsican hellebore)
FLOWER COLOUR Pinkish green
FLOWERING TIME Late winter to early spring
HEIGHT 90 cm
DESCRIPTION Valued for its evergreen foliage and its beautiful cup-shaped flowers. It looks wonderful when left to naturalise under trees.
CULTIVATION Plant in soil that has been enriched with organic matter. Helleborus prefer dappled shade.
PROPAGATION Seed sown in spring or by root division in late autumn.
OTHER SPECIES The subspecies *corsicus* has yellowish green flowers.

Helleborus niger (Christmas rose)
FLOWER COLOUR White becoming pink with age
FLOWERING TIME Winter
HEIGHT 20–40 cm
DESCRIPTION The white flowers look striking against the leathery evergreen leaves. Plant in drifts under trees.
CULTIVATION Grow in full or semi-shade in a rich, well-drained soil that has been enriched with organic matter.
PROPAGATION Seed when they ripen or by root division in autumn. If the plants are left alone they will readily self-seed.

Helleborus x orientalis (Lenten rose)
FLOWER COLOUR Shades of purple, pink, crimson, white or cream
FLOWERING TIME Late winter to spring
HEIGHT 45 cm
DESCRIPTION The Lenten rose grows well among trees or shrubs as a low-maintenance groundcover. It has leathery, dark green leaves and each flower stem carries several cup-shaped flowers.
CULTIVATION Grow in full or dappled shade in a rich, well-drained soil that has been enriched with organic matter to help retain soil moisture.
PROPAGATION Seed when they ripen or by root division during autumn.

Hemerocallis hybrids (daylily)
FLOWER COLOUR There are hundreds of different varieties in most colours. Flowers are usually tinted towards the centre with another colour and the petals may be marked or blushed with deeper or lighter contrasting shades.
FLOWERING TIME Summer
HEIGHT 1 m
DESCRIPTION Fibrous-rooted perennials having strap-like leaves. Although each flower only lasts for one day there are 7–8 flowers on each stalk so that one stalk may flower for a week or more.
CULTIVATION Grow in sun or light shade in rich, well-drained garden soil. They are hardy perennials that will compete strongly if not given sufficient room. Grow them in a bed of their own or leave space each side if they are planted next to shrubs. Divide every three years if required.
PROPAGATION Division in autumn.
CULTIVARS Hundreds of named varieties.

Heterocentron elegans (Spanish shawl, trailing lasiandra)
FLOWER COLOUR Magenta
FLOWERING TIME Summer to autumn

HEIGHT 5 cm
DESCRIPTION The pretty flowers virtually cover the small foliage and reddish brown stems. Spanish shawl will spread up to 45 cm, rooting along its stems.
CULTIVATION In warm or hot climates plant in a lightly shaded position. In cooler climates it will tolerate sun.
PROPAGATION Separate the rooted stems at any time or take short tip cuttings during spring.

Heuchera sanguinea (coral bells)
FLOWER COLOUR Bright red
FLOWERING TIME Spring to mid-summer
HEIGHT 50 cm
DESCRIPTION The delicate flowers are borne on 30 cm high slender stems. The heart-shaped leaves form a tuft.
CULTIVATION Grow in full sun and in a moist but well-drained soil. It is a hardy plant that looks good in a rockery or a border alongside a path.
PROPAGATION Division during winter.
CULTIVARS 'Alba' has white flowers. 'Maxima' has dark crimson flowers. 'Red Spangles' has scarlet flowers.

Hibbertia serpyllifolia (Guinea flower)
FLOWER COLOUR Yellow
FLOWERING TIME Most of the year
HEIGHT 10 cm
DESCRIPTION The brightly coloured flowers almost cover the small, dark green foliage. Use as a groundcover or allow it to drape over a wall.
CULTIVATION Guinea flower thrives in well-drained soil in a lightly shaded position. It is a hardy plant requiring minimal maintenance.
PROPAGATION Summer cuttings.

Hosta plantaginea (plantain lily)
FLOWER COLOUR White
FLOWERING TIME Summer
HEIGHT 30 cm
DESCRIPTION The sweetly-scented flowers arise among the light green, oval-shaped foliage. The leaves die down during winter. Grow as an accent plant in the cottage garden or under trees.
CULTIVATION Hostas like a soil that has been enriched with organic matter and a position in light or dappled shade. Protect from snails and slugs in early spring when the new growth appears.
PROPAGATION Root division in autumn.
OTHER SPECIES *H. fortunei* has lance-like leaves. *H. sieboldiana* has metallic blue foliage. *H. caerulea* has long, narrow foliage. *H. lancifolia* has narrow, lance-like foliage.

Houstonia caerulea (blue cushion)
FLOWER COLOUR Blue to white
FLOWERING TIME Spring
HEIGHT 15 cm
DESCRIPTION The small, salver-form flowers virtually cover the tiny bright green leaves.
CULTIVATION Grow blue cushion in light shade and in rich, moist but well-drained soil.
PROPAGATION Division at any time of the year.
OTHER SPECIES *H. purpurea* has purple flowers.

Incarvillea delavayi (pride of China)
FLOWER COLOUR Dark pink
FLOWERING TIME Summer
HEIGHT 60 cm
DESCRIPTION The wide trumpet-shaped flowers appear above the attractive, shiny, pinnate foliage. A pretty plant for the herbaceous border.
CULTIVATION An easily grown perennial that can be left undisturbed for years. Grow in full sun and in rich, organic soil. Keep mulched during the summer months.
PROPAGATION Root division in winter.
OTHER SPECIES *I. lutea* has yellow flowers.

Kniphofia hybrids (red hot poker)
FLOWER COLOUR Varying degrees of red and yellow
FLOWERING TIME Spring to summer
HEIGHT 50 cm
DESCRIPTION The tall flower spikes rise above the thin, strap-like leaves. Grow on banks or at the back of the border.
CULTIVATION Red hot pokers prefer full sun and a free-draining soil. Apply a complete fertiliser in early spring.
PROPAGATION Division in autumn.
CULTIVARS Numerous named and unnamed varieties are available.

Lavatera trimestris (tree mallow)
FLOWER COLOUR Rosy-pink
FLOWERING TIME Summer
HEIGHT 90 cm

THE LARGE LEAVES OF HOSTAS ARE INDISPENSABLE IN AN ANNUAL AND PERENNIAL GARDEN

DESCRIPTION A quick-growing herbaceous perennial with trumpet-shaped flowers and heart-shaped foliage. A good background plant for the herbaceous border.
CULTIVATION Plant in full sun and a well-drained, fertile soil. Cut the flower stems back when they have finished flowering.
PROPAGATION Seed sown in spring.
CULTIVARS 'Alba' has white flowers. 'Splendens' has pink flowers.

Liatris spicata (gayfeather)
FLOWER COLOUR Pinkish purple
FLOWERING TIME Summer to autumn
HEIGHT 1 m
DESCRIPTION The tall flower spikes appear above the clumps of linear foliage. Plant in clumps in the herbaceous border.
CULTIVATION Gayfeather prefers a position in full sun in a well-drained but fertile soil.
PROPAGATION Division of the roots in winter.
CULTIVARS There are white and lavender forms available.

Limonium latifolium (perennial statice)
FLOWER COLOUR Lavender-blue
FLOWERING TIME Spring to summer
HEIGHT 50 cm
DESCRIPTION The tall stems carry panicles of long-lasting flowers above tufts of large, elliptical leaves.
CULTIVATION Grow in full sun in a well-drained, fertile soil.
PROPAGATION Root division in winter.
OTHER SPECIES *L. perezii* has broad, basal leaves and bluish purple flowers.

Lupinus polyphyllus 'Russell Lupins' (lupins)
FLOWER COLOUR Depends on the variety
FLOWERING TIME Summer
HEIGHT 1.5 m
DESCRIPTION A pretty perennial with soft green leaflets and erect stems which bear dense racemes of pea-like flowers.
CULTIVATION Sun-loving plants which thrive in well-drained, alkaline soil. Cut back to the

basal clump after flowering and mulch in autumn.
PROPAGATION Division of the root crown or basal cuttings in spring.
CULTIVARS There are many different named varieties in a variety of flower colours.

Lychnis coronaria (rose campion)
FLOWER COLOUR Bright magenta
FLOWERING TIME Late spring and summer
HEIGHT 50–60 cm
DESCRIPTION The pretty open flowers look magnificent next to the grey foliage. Grow in the border for colour contrast.
CULTIVATION Grow this hardy plant in full sun and well-drained soil that has been enriched with organic matter. Once rose campion has been introduced to the garden it will readily self-seed.
PROPAGATION Division in spring.
CULTIVARS 'Alba' has white flowers. 'Atrosanguinea' produces crimson flowers. 'Ocellata' has white flowers with a pink centre.
OTHER SPECIES *L. chalcedonica* has bright scarlet flowers *L. chalcedonica* 'Rosea' has pink flowers.

Lythrum salicaria (purple loosestrife)
FLOWER COLOUR Purple
FLOWERING TIME Summer and autumn
HEIGHT 1.5 m
DESCRIPTION The square, branched stems hold lanceolate leaves and terminal spikes which bear whorled clusters of flowers.
CULTIVATION A hardy perennial for badly drained soil. It will grow in well-drained soil but appreciates copious amounts of water during summer. Cut the stems back to ground level after flowering.
PROPAGATION By division or cuttings during spring.

Malva moschata (musk mallow)
FLOWER COLOUR Rose-pink
FLOWERING TIME Summer to autumn
HEIGHT 60 cm
DESCRIPTION The large open flowers look most attractive next to the deeply lobed leaves. An old cottage garden favourite.
CULTIVATION Plant in a sunny position and in well-drained soil. Dig a complete plant food into the soil when planting.
PROPAGATION Seed sown in spring.
OTHER SPECIES *M. alcea* has pink-purple flowers in summer and autumn.

Meconopsis betonicifolia (Himalayan blue poppy)
FLOWER COLOUR Blue
FLOWERING TIME Late spring to early summer
HEIGHT 90–120 cm
DESCRIPTION Grown for its beautiful, large, poppy-like flowers and grey-green foliage.
CULTIVATION The Himalayan poppy is not easy to grow but is certainly worth a try. For best results it must be planted in semi-shade and in moist but well-drained soil. Dig copious amounts of compost or cow manure into the soil before planting. When it dies down over winter you should take care not to over-water. If you want it to remain as a perennial, it is advisable not to let it flower in the first year by removing buds. It is suitable for cold climates only.
PROPAGATION Seed sown in spring.
OTHER SPECIES *M. cambrica* bears large yellow flowers and is very easy to grow. Remove the buds in the first season if you want it to remain as a perennial. It is capable of self-seeding.

Nepeta x faassenii (catmint)
FLOWER COLOUR Mauve
FLOWERING TIME Spring to autumn
HEIGHT 40 cm
DESCRIPTION Catmint is an aromatic border and edging plant. It has greyish green leaves and racemes of lipped , mauve flowers.
CULTIVATION Plant catmint in well-drained soil and a sunny or lightly shaded position. Trim back the old flowering stems in early spring as the new growth appears from the crown.
PROPAGATION Propagate by seed or cutting in spring.
OTHER SPECIES *N. cataria* bears whorls of mauve-dotted, white flowers in summer

Oenothera biennis (evening primrose)
FLOWER COLOUR Yellow
FLOWERING TIME Summer
HEIGHT 1 m
DESCRIPTION The large, cup-shaped flowers open in the late afternoon and shine through

the night. It has a bushy habit.
CULTIVATION Plant in full sun and in fertile soil. Apply a complete plant food in late spring. It is actually a biennial plant but if cut back after flowering it will bloom again the following year.
PROPAGATION Seed sown in spring. Once introduced into the garden it will readily self-seed but can be kept in check by weeding.
OTHER SPECIES *O. acaulis* has white flowers which age to pink. *O. odorata* is the true evening primrose with deep yellow flowers which fill the evening air with fragrance. *O. pallida* has fragrant white flowers which often mature to pink. *O. speciosa* has pink flowers which appear during the day.

Ophiopogon japonicus (mondo grass)
FLOWER COLOUR Violet-pink
FLOWERING TIME Summer
HEIGHT 30 cm
DESCRIPTION Grown for its tufted, grass-like leaves and racemes of flowers. It makes an ideal garden border or groundcover or can be used as a lawn in light traffic areas.
CULTIVATION A handy perennial as it will grow in light or heavy shade and is tolerant of most soil conditions. For best results plant in soil that has been enriched with organic matter.
PROPAGATION Division at any time of the year.

Oxalis magellanica (oxalis)
FLOWER COLOUR Pink
FLOWERING TIME Spring to summer
HEIGHT 10–15 cm
DESCRIPTION Grown for its tri-foliate bronze leaves and pretty flowers. Grow as a groundcover or in a container.
CULTIVATION Grow in a shady position in a moist but well-drained soil. Dig in manure or compost before planting.
PROPAGATION Division in early winter.
OTHER SPECIES *O. acetosella* has white flowers. *O. versicolor* has white flowers that are margined with red and yellow.

Paeonia lactifolia (Chinese peony)
FLOWER COLOUR White or pink
FLOWERING TIME Early summer
HEIGHT 1 m
DESCRIPTION An herbaceous perennial that has a thickened root stock from which new growth appears. It dies back during winter. The large flowers look magnificent against the attractive foliage.
CULTIVATION Grow in semi-shade in a cold climate. The soil should be enriched with organic matter and should be moist but well-drained. Leave the plants undisturbed once they have been planted.
PROPAGATION Layering, cutting or seed in spring.
CULTIVARS There are many different varieties.

Paeonia suffruticosa (tree peony)
FLOWER COLOUR White, creamy-yellow, shades of pink, red, crimson or rosy-purple depending on the variety
FLOWERING TIME Early summer
HEIGHT 2 m
DESCRIPTION Valued for its large flowers and large compound leaves. Grow in a mixed border.
CULTIVATION Likes a position in semi-shade, a cold climate and a rich, moist soil.
PROPAGATION By grafting or budding onto seedling stock.
CULTIVARS There are many different varieties having single and double flowers.

Papaver orientale (oriental poppy)
FLOWER COLOUR Red with a black centre but other coloured varieties include pink, white and orange
FLOWERING TIME Late spring to early summer
HEIGHT 60–90 cm
DESCRIPTION The oriental poppy is admired for its large flowers and attractive grey-green foliage. It is a hardy perennial that dies down during winter. Suitable for cold climates.
CULTIVATION Grow in a sunny position in a rich, well-drained soil. Add organic matter to the soil before planting. Oriental poppy usually takes more than one year to flower.
PROPAGATION Division in autumn.

Pelargonium x domesticum (regal pelargonium)
FLOWER COLOUR Shades of pink, purple, maroon or white
FLOWERING TIME Spring to summer
HEIGHT 1 m
DESCRIPTION Grown for their large flowers

PINK EVENING PRIMROSE (*OENOTHERA SPECIOSA*)

which are usually marked with contrasting colours and fragrant foliage. They are hardy plants that can be grown in tubs, on banks or in borders.
CULTIVATION Regal pelargoniums like a light, free-draining soil, a frost-free climate and a position in full sun.
PROPAGATION Cuttings taken in summer
CULTIVARS *P. fragrans* has nutmeg-scented leaves and white flowers. *P. graveolens* has rose-scented leaves. *P. odoratissimum* has apple-scented leaves. *P. quercifolium* has large hairy leaves and rosy-pink flowers.
P. peltatum is commmonly called the ivy-leaf geranium because of its ivy-shaped leaves.

Pelargonium x hortorum (zonal geranium)
FLOWER COLOUR Shades of orange, purple, red, apricot, pink or white
FLOWERING TIME Spring to summer
HEIGHT 1 m
DESCRIPTION Grown for their attractively marked foliage as well as their flowers. Grow in the perennial border, in pots or on banks.

CULTIVATION For best results plant in a light, free-draining sandy soil and a position in full sun.
PROPAGATION Summer cuttings.
CULTIVARS There are hundreds of different varieties, many of which have scented leaves.

Penstemon hybrids
FLOWER COLOUR Pink, purple, off-white or crimson
FLOWERING TIME Summer
HEIGHT 60–90 cm
DESCRIPTION The tall flower spikes arise above the mound of narrow-leafed green foliage. A pretty cottage garden plant.
CULTIVATION Full sun and a well-drained soil that has been enriched with organic matter will give good results with this plant. Cut back the flowers after they have finished.
PROPAGATION Division of the roots during winter or seed sown in late summer-early autumn.
OTHER SPECIES *P. barbatus* bears nodding, two-lipped, red flowers with yellow beards, in

PINK AND ORANGE ORIENTAL POPPIES (*PAPAVER ORIENTALE*)

spring and summer. *P. digitalis* has pink-lavender or white foxglove-like flowers during spring and summer. *P. hartwegii* is the parent of many popular hybrids. *P. hirsutus* has lavender-purple flowers.

Phlox paniculata (perennial phlox)
FLOWER COLOUR White, mauve, orange, purple, rose-pink, salmon or crimson depending on the variety
FLOWERING TIME Summer to autumn
HEIGHT 75–150 cm
DESCRIPTION Valued for its colourful heads of flowers. A pretty cottage garden plant suitable for the herbaceous border.
CULTIVATION Grow in full sun or light shade and in soil that has been enriched with cow manure or compost.
PROPAGATION Division or root cuttings during winter.
CULTIVARS There are many different varieties, some with plain colours and some with contrasting colours.

Phlox subulata (alpine or moss phlox)
FLOWER COLOUR White, crimson, blue, pink or red depending on the variety
FLOWERING TIME Spring
HEIGHT 15 cm
DESCRIPTION The five-petalled, simple flowers completely cover the mat-like, green foliage in spring. Use in rock gardens or plant between stones on pathways or courtyards.
CULTIVATION Alpine phlox likes full sun and fertile, well-drained soil. It prefers cooler climates. Keep well-watered during summer.
PROPAGATION Alpine phlox sends out runners which root easily. These can be detached from the parent plant in late winter.
CULTIVARS There are many different varieties.

Physostegia virginiana (obedient plant)
FLOWER COLOUR Mauve-pink
FLOWERING TIME Summer to autumn
HEIGHT 1 m
DESCRIPTION A hardy perennial which forms a dense clump. The bell-like flowers appear on

tall spikes. Obedient plant looks delightful in a cottage garden or can be grown as a fill-in plant between shrubs.
CULTIVATION Obedient plant will grow in sun or light shade, although the flowers are a deeper colour when given some shade. The soil should be rich in organic matter. Mulch around the roots with grass clippings or leaf mould to keep the soil moist.
PROPAGATION Division in late autumn.
CULTIVARS 'Alba' has white flowers. 'Bouquet Rose' has deep pink flowers. 'Rosea' has rose-pink flowers. 'Speciosa' has pale pink flowers. 'Vivid' has rosy red flowers.

Platycodon grandiflorum (balloon flower)
FLOWER COLOUR Blue
FLOWERING TIME Summer
HEIGHT 50–60 cm
DESCRIPTION The pretty, open, bell-like flowers appear at the top of the stems. Balloon flower forms a large clump but dies down during winter.
CULTIVATION Grow in a position in full sun except in hot climates where it prefers partial shade.
PROPAGATION Root division in winter or seed sown in spring.
CULTIVARS 'Album' has white flowers. 'Roseum' has rosy-lilac flowers. 'Mother of Pearl' has semi-double pink flowers.

Plectranthus ecklonii (cockspur flower)
FLOWER COLOUR Purple
FLOWERING TIME Autumn
HEIGHT 30 cm
DESCRIPTION The purple flowers sit above bright green foliage. It is a hardy plant that will often grow in a position where nothing else will grow.
CULTIVATION Grow in sun or semi-shade in any type of garden soil.
PROPAGATION Root division in autumn or winter.
OTHER SPECIES *P. oertendahlii* has an attractive trailing habit. The dark green, purple-backed leaves are topped with delicate sprays of white flowers.

Polemonium caeruleum (Jacob's ladder)
FLOWER COLOUR Violet-blue
FLOWERING TIME Spring to summer
HEIGHT 80 cm
DESCRIPTION The pretty flowers arise from a clump of slender stems bearing alternate leaflets similar in appearance to the steps of a ladder.
CULTIVATION Grow Jacob's ladder in moist but well-drained soil, in sun or partial shade. Water well in dry weather.
PROPAGATION By division in autumn or seed in spring.
OTHER SPECIES *P. boreale* reaches a height of 20 cm and has blue flowers. *P. carneum* has silky, flesh-pink flowers in summer. *P. foliosissimum* produces deep violet flowers with orange stamens.

Polygonatum multifolium (Solomon's seal)
FLOWER COLOUR White
FLOWERING TIME Spring
HEIGHT 1 m
DESCRIPTION A pretty plant for shaded areas of the garden. During spring the white flowers hang off tall stems.
CULTIVATION Solomon's seal likes a cool, moist but well-drained soil.
PROPAGATION Division in winter.
OTHER SPECIES *P. x hybridum* has greeny-white flowers. *P. odoratum* has scented flowers, as the name suggests.

Polygonum bistorta (polygonum)
FLOWER COLOUR White or pink
FLOWERING TIME Summer
HEIGHT 60 cm
DESCRIPTION An attractive plant for an herbaceous border. The flowers appear on oblong spikes.
CULTIVATION Polygonum is tolerant of most soil types but appreciates a soil that has been enriched with organic matter. It will grow in sun or semi-shade.
PROPAGATION Cuttings in spring or division of the roots.
CULTIVARS 'Superbum' has bright pink flowers.
OTHER SPECIES *P. affine* is an ideal groundcover for areas where it is often difficult to get anything else to grow. The pink flowers appear throughout autumn.

Primula x polyantha (polyanthus)
FLOWER COLOUR Large colour range
FLOWERING TIME Early winter to spring
HEIGHT 25 cm
DESCRIPTION Grown for their beautiful salver-form primrose-like flowers and rosettes of

WHITE PENSTEMON

bright green leaves.
CULTIVATION Polyanthus prefer full or semi-shade but will grow in the sun. They are often treated as annuals but if left in the garden they will multiply each year. Polyanthus prefer a friable soil that has been enriched with organic matter.
PROPAGATION Division when they are dormant or seed sown in late summer and early autumn.
CULTIVARS 'Pacific Giants' has a superb colour range.
OTHER SPECIES *P. auricula* has dense umbels of large, fragrant yellow flowers. *P. denticulata* is a tall primrose having pinkish purple, yellow-eyed flowers. *P. elatior* bears an abundance of yellow flowers. *P. florindae* thrives in moist soil and has bright yellow, scented flowers. *P. japonica* has magenta, white or rose flowers. *P. obconica* produces umbels of lilac to pink flowers. *P. sinensis*, commonly called the Chinese primrose, has very large flowers in many colours. *P. vulgaris* is the English primrose.

Pulmonaria officinalis (medicinal lungwort)
FLOWER COLOUR Pinkish purple
FLOWERING TIME Spring
HEIGHT 30 cm
DESCRIPTION The plant derives its common name from its former use as a treatment for lung problems. It has hairy, green, lanceolate leaves and its funnel-shaped flowers change to blue as they mature.
CULTIVATION Lungwort likes a cool, moist soil and a shady situation. Mulch with manure or compost in early spring.
PROPAGATION By division.

Pulsatilla vulgaris syn. *Anemone vulgaris* (pasque flower)
FLOWER COLOUR Purplish-blue
FLOWERING TIME Spring
HEIGHT 30–40 cm
DESCRIPTION The extremely pretty, 6-petalled flowers sit above the fern-like foliage. Grow in clumps in the herbaceous border.
CULTIVATION Pasque flower thrives in sun or semi-shade in soil previously enriched with organic matter. It likes moist but well-drained conditions. Mulch during summer with leaf mould or grass clippings to help retain moisture.
PROPAGATION Division in winter
CULTIVARS There is a red-flowering form.

THE PRETTY PINK FLOWERS OF POLYGONUM

Rehmannia elata (Beverly bells)
FLOWER COLOUR Purplish-pink
FLOWERING TIME Spring to autumn
HEIGHT 90 cm
DESCRIPTION Rehmannia is valued for its long flowering period. The large bell-like flowers complement the soft, green, hairy foliage.
CULTIVATION Rehmannia will grow in semi-shade but prefers sun. The soil should be well-drained and rich in organic matter. It dies down in winter in cold climates but remains evergreen throughout the year in warm areas.
PROPAGATION Division in winter.
CULTIVARS Cream and pink forms are available.

Romneya coulteri (Californian tree poppy)
FLOWER COLOUR White
FLOWERING TIME Mid-summer to early autumn
HEIGHT 1–1.5 m

BEVERLY BELLS (*REHMANNIA ELATA*)

DESCRIPTION A pretty, bushy perennial that looks magnificent planted at the back of an herbaceous border. The deeply lobed leaves are blue-green.
CULTIVATION Plant in full sun in light, well-drained soil that has been enriched previously with organic matter. Once romneyas are established in the garden they are best left undisturbed as they resent root disturbance. In late autumn cut the stems down to 10 cm above ground level.
PROPAGATION Sow seed when ripe or take 8–10 cm root cuttings in late winter.

Rudbeckia fulgida (cone flower)
FLOWER COLOUR Yellow with brown centre disc
FLOWERING TIME Summer to autumn
HEIGHT 1.5 m
DESCRIPTION Valued for its long flowering period, rapid growth and its abundance of flowers. The leaves are mid-green. Makes an excellent cut flower.
CULTIVATION Cone flower prefers a sunny position and a medium to sandy loam with compost added. It is an excellent plant for growing near the sea. Keep well-watered during summer. Give fortnightly feeds of a soluble complete fertiliser when the buds appear.
PROPAGATION Division of an established clump in late winter or early spring. Seed sown in spring or early summer.
CULTIVARS 'Goldsturm' has larger flowers.
OTHER SPECIES *R. californica* has yellow flowers with a raised greenish yellow centre.

Salvia azurea (blue sage)
FLOWER COLOUR Blue
FLOWERING TIME Summer to autumn
HEIGHT 70 cm
DESCRIPTION The spikes of blue flowers highlight the grey-green foliage. It makes a delightful contrast plant among predominantly green-leaved plants.
CULTIVATION Blue sage prefers full sun. The soil should be free-draining and on the dry side. Fertilise monthly during spring and summer with a complete plant food.

PROPAGATION Seed sown in spring.
OTHER SPECIES *S. argentea* has large, white, woolly leaves and white flowers. *S. coccinea* has bright scarlet flowers. *S. elegans*, commonly called pineapple sage, has scarlet flowers during autumn. *S. farinacea* has purple flowers. *S. leucantha* is a durable species, with white woolly stems and leaves and purple flowers. *S. officinalis* is the well known common sage used in cooking. There are many different varieties of this species. *S. patens* has beautiful large, blue flowers. *S. sclarea* has woolly and aromatic leaves and spikes of pale blue flowers during summer and autumn. *S. uliginosa* is tolerant of wet soils and shade.

Sanguisorba canadensis (Canadian burnet)
FLOWER COLOUR White
FLOWERING TIME Summer
HEIGHT 1.2 m
DESCRIPTION The mid-green leaves are toothed and divided. The flowers are borne on 10 cm long cylindrical spikes with protruding stamens which give the flower a fluffy appearance similar to a bottlebrush.
CULTIVATION Grow in a sunny situation in moist but well-drained soil. Water abundantly during the growing season. Mulch with cow manure or compost in late winter.
PROPAGATION Divide and replant the roots in early spring or sow seed in autumn.
OTHER SPECIES *S. obtusa* has rose-crimson flowers during summer.

Santolina chamaecyparissus (cotton lavender)
FLOWER COLOUR Yellow
FLOWERING TIME Summer
HEIGHT 60 cm
DESCRIPTION Valued for its silver, finely dissected leaves and dainty, button-like flowers. Grow as a low clipped hedge around the herb garden or as an accent plant between shrubs.
CULTIVATION Cotton lavender will grow in any well-drained soil and a position in full sun. Apply a light mulch of compost or manure in early spring.
PROPAGATION Take cuttings 5–8 cm long in mid to late summer.

Saponaria officinalis (soap wort)
FLOWER COLOUR Pink
FLOWERING TIME Summer
HEIGHT 30–60 cm
DESCRIPTION A hardy perennial with pale green, oblong-lanceolate leaves. Grow in the herbaceous border.
CULTIVATION Suitable for sun or partial shade in any fertile garden soil. Incorporate manure or compost into the soil before planting.
PROPAGATION Divide the roots in autumn or spring.
CULTIVARS 'Alba-plena' has white flowers. 'Rosea-plena' displays pink flowers.

Saxifraga umbrosa (London pride)
FLOWER COLOUR Pink
FLOWERING TIME Spring and early summer
HEIGHT 30–45 cm
DESCRIPTION A dainty perennial best suited to cool, moist soils. It has rosettes of slightly fleshy, thick, mid to dark green leaves. The loose panicles of small, pink starry flowers are carried on 45 cm stems above the foliage.
CULTIVATION London pride prefers an alkaline, fertile soil that is free-draining. A position in dappled sun or semi-shade is suitable.
PROPAGATION Divide plants after flowering.

Silene dioica (red campion)
FLOWER COLOUR Deep pink
FLOWERING TIME Spring and summer
HEIGHT 60 cm
DESCRIPTION The pretty open flowers are carried in profusion for a long period. A delightful cottage garden plant. Red campion spreads widely by self-sown seedlings.
CULTIVATION Red campion will grow in full sun or semi-shade.
PROPAGATION Sow seed in early spring.
OTHER SPECIES *S. vulgaris* has white, star-like flowers which have a balloon-like calyx. It will spread rapidly throughout the garden. *S. vulgaris* ssp. *maritima* forms a mat of grey-green leaves and has white flowers.

Solidago canadense (golden rod)
FLOWER COLOUR Yellow
FLOWERING TIME Summer to autumn
HEIGHT 1.5 m
DESCRIPTION A vigorous herbaceous perennial

with mid-green leaves and heads of tiny, yellow clustered flowers.
CULTIVATION A position in full sun or partial shade and any good garden soil is sutiable for this plant. This species is very invasive and the hybrids are more commonly grown.
PROPAGATION Divide and replant roots in late autumn or early spring.
CULTIVARS S. x 'Golden Wings' reaches a height of 1.5 m. S. x 'Golden Thumb' only reaches a height of 30 cm.

Stachys byzantina (lamb's ears, woolly betony)
FLOWER COLOUR Rosy purple
FLOWERING TIME Summer and autumn
HEIGHT 45 cm
DESCRIPTION Grown for its thick silvery foliage which is velvety to the touch. The flowers appear on small spikes.
CULTIVATION Grow in an open, sunny position in well-drained, friable soil. Mulch in early spring with cow manure or compost.
PROPAGATION Division during winter or cuttings taken in spring or summer.
OTHER SPECIES *S. grandiflora* will tolerate some shade. *S. officinalis* has green leaves and rosy-purple flowers.

Stokesia laevis (Stoke's aster)
FLOWER COLOUR Mauve
FLOWERING TIME Summer to early autumn
HEIGHT 60 cm
DESCRIPTION A useful, long-flowering perennial for garden show or cut flowers. It has long, lance-like leaves.
CULTIVATION Stoke's aster prefers a sunny, open position and well-drained, rich garden soil.
PROPAGATION Division of the clump in late winter or early spring.
CULTIVARS 'Lilacina' has lilac-blue flowers. 'Rosea' has rose pink flowers. 'Alba has white flowers.

Thalictrum dipterocarpum (lavender shower)
FLOWER COLOUR Mauve
FLOWERING TIME Spring and summer
HEIGHT 120–180 cm
DESCRIPTION An extremely elegant perennial having deeply divided leaves that look very similar to maidenhair fern. The small flowers are borne on loose panicles and have conspicuous yellow anthers.
CULTIVATION Grow in rich, moist soil that is topdressed annually with manure or compost. A position in sun or semi-shade will produce good results.
PROPAGATION Seed sown in spring.
OTHER SPECIES *T. aquilegifolium* has rosy-purple flowers. The flowers have no petals but many showy stamens. *T. speciosissimum* has large panicles of fluffy, yellow flowers.

Thymus serpyllum (wild or creeping thyme)
FLOWER COLOUR Deep lilac
FLOWERING TIME Late spring and summer
HEIGHT 10 cm
DESCRIPTION A creeping plant that makes an ideal groundcover. The leaves and flowers are perfumed. Grow between large stones in a pathway.
CULTIVATION Suited to any garden soil in a position of full sun. An occasional trim will keep plants tidy.
PROPAGATION Division in early spring or autumn.
CULTIVARS 'Aureus' has golden foliage. 'Albus' has white flowers. 'Coccineus' has crimson flowers. 'Magic Carpet' has lilac-pink flowers. 'Annie Hall' has pink flowers.
OTHER SPECIES *T. citriodorus* has rosy-mauve flowers. *T. citriodorus* 'Aureus' has lemon-scented variegated foliage. *T. pseudolanguinosus* has lilac-pink flowers. *T. vulgaris* is the well-known garden thyme.

Verbascum chaixii 'Album' (mullein)
FLOWER COLOUR White with a mauve eye
FLOWERING TIME Summer
HEIGHT 1 m
DESCRIPTION A stately perennial which has a rosette of ovate, long, grey-green leaves and slender flower spires.
CULTIVATION Mullein thrives in well-drained, dry soil and full sun. It is short-lived but will often self-seed.
PROPAGATION By seed or division in spring.
OTHER SPECIES *V. chaixii* has pale yellow flowers. *V. bombyciferum*, commonly called

Red campion (*Silene dioica*)

woolly mullein, is a biennial which grows from a rosette of huge, felty-white leaves.

Verbena x hybrida (verbena)
FLOWER COLOUR Salmon, rose, red, lavender or white depending on the variety
FLOWERING TIME Spring and summer
HEIGHT 40–50 cm
DESCRIPTION The compact heads of colourful flowers make this a popular perennial. It is often grown as an annual.
CULTIVATION Grow in a fertile, well-drained soil enriched with manure or compost. A position in full sun is preferred but verbena is tolerant of semi-shade. Plants may be kept bushy by pinching out new shoots.
PROPAGATION Seed may be sown in all the warm months from spring until autumn.
OTHER SPECIES *V. officinalis* has pink flowers in summer. *V. rigida* has purple flowers.

Veronica spicata (speedwell)
FLOWER COLOUR Blue
FLOWERING TIME Spring and summer
HEIGHT 40 cm
DESCRIPTION The 15 cm flower spikes rise above the mat of dark green, lanceolate leaves. Speedwell makes a pretty groundcover.
CULTIVATION Speedwell prefers an open sunny position and will grow in any soil type. For best results enrich the soil with organic matter before planting.
PROPAGATION Division of plants in autumn or spring. Soft tip cuttings in spring and summer.
CULTIVARS There are many named varieties in white and shades of pink and blue.

Viola odorata (sweet violet)
FLOWER COLOUR Reddish purple, violet purple, dark violet, rose pink, deep violet, blue or white depending on the variety
FLOWERING TIME Spring
HEIGHT 5–10 cm
DESCRIPTION The sweetly scented flowers appear among broadly-ovate leaves. Violets make an ideal groundcover, especially if they are left to naturalise beneath trees.
CULTIVATION Grow in sun or shade in a rich, organic, well-drained soil. In late winter add a top-dressing of manure or compost around the plants. Give plenty of water in hot weather.
PROPAGATION Division in spring.
CULTIVARS There are hundreds of named varieties in white and shades of blue, pink and purple.
OTHER SPECIES *V. hederacea* has violet-blue and white flowers.

Index

Acanthus longifolius 31, 139
Acanthus mollis 19, 69, 82, 139
Acanthus montanus 139
Acanthus spinosissimus 139
Achillea 34
Achillea ageratum 139
Achillea filipendulina 31, 139
Achillea grandiflora 139
Achillea millefolium 31, 33, 139
Achillea millefolium 'Cerise Queen' 139
Achillea millefolium 'Rosea' 139
Achillea ptarmica 139
Achillea tomentosa 31
Aconitum fischeri 140
Aconitum napellus 33, 82, 140
Actinotus helianthi 32
Agastache foeniculum 140
Agastache mexicana 140
Ageratum houstonianum 119
Agrostemma githago 'Milas' 58, 119
Ajuga reptans 26, 82, 140
Alcea rosea 31, 33, 69, 140
Alchemilla mollis 140
Alkanet 141
Allwood pink 148
Alonsoa warscewiczii 141
Alpine phlox 162
Alstroemeria aurea 31, 82, 141
Alstroemeria pulchella 141
Althea officinalis 141
Alyssum 58, 129
Alyssum saxatile 144
Alyssum, yellow 144
Amaranthus caudatus 119
Amaranthus hybridus 119
Ammi majus 48, 54, 120
Anchusa azurea 141
Anchusa capensis 141
Anchusa capensis 'Blue Bird' 46
Anchusa officinalis 141
Anemone blanda 31, 33, 82, 84, 141

Anemone x hybrida 31, 33, 77, 82, 84, 142
Anemone, Japanese 84
Anemone vulgaris 165
Anemone, woodland 141
Angelica archangelica 94
Anise 93
Anthemis montana 73
Anthemis nobilis 31, 73
Antirrhinum majus 63, 120
Aquilegia alpina 143
Aquilegia caerulea 143
Aquilegia flabellata 33, 143
Aquilegia vulgaris 31, 33, 54, 82, 142
Aquilegia x hybrida 31, 143
Arabis albida 31
Arabis caucasica 143
Arenaria balearica 143
Arenaria montana 31, 143
Argemone hispida 143
Armeria maritima 32, 143
Armeria pseudarmeria 'Giant White' 143
Armeria pseudarmeria 'Rubra' 143
Artemisia absinthium 32, 77, 94, 143
Artemisia frigida 143
Artemisia lactiflora 31, 94, 143
Aster alpinus 144
Aster amellus 144
Aster laevis 144
Aster novi-belgii hybrids 31, 33, 69, 143
Aster x frikartii 144
Astilbe chinensis 144
Astilbe x arendsii 18, 31, 33, 82, 144
Astrantia major 144
Astrantia maxima 144
Aubrieta deltoidea 144
Aurinia saxatilis 31, 144

Babies' tears 54, 72, 76, 89, 152
Baby blue eyes 131
Baby's breath 126, 155
Balloon flower 163
Balsam 126
Basil 93

Bay 93
Bear's breeches 139
Beech 51
Bee plant 152
Bellis perennis 33, 82, 98, 144
Bells of Ireland 46, 130
Bergamot 94
Bergenia x schmidtii 33, 82, 145
Betula pendula 51
Beverly bells 165
Bleeding heart 150
Bloody crane's bill 155
Bluebells of Scotland 145
Blue cushion 157
Blue daisy 23, 27, 72, 89, 153
Blue fescue 14, 59
Blue marguerite 153
Blue thimble flower 125
Borage 93
Brachycome angustifolia 145
Brachycome iberdifolia 14, 72, 89
Brachycome multifida 33, 145
Brown sedge 14, 59
Brunnera macrophylla 33, 145
Bugle weed 26, 140
Burning bush 150
Busy Lizzie 54, 128
Butterfly delphinium 19

Calendula officinalis 23, 34, 88, 100, 120
Californian bluebell 46, 133
Californian poppy 34, 54, 124
Californian tree poppy 165
Callistephus chinensis 121
Calonyction aculeatum 76
Campanula barbata 146
Campanula carpatica 146
Campanula glomerata 146
Campanula isophylla 33, 82, 145
Campanula isophylla 'Alba' 145
Campanula latifolia 16, 27, 146

Campanula medium 16, 27, 31, 33, 69, 82, 121
Campanula persicifolia 27, 145
Campanula persicifolia 'Sessiflora'
Campanula poscharskyana 27, 180
Campanula portenschlagiana 33, 145
Campanula pyramidalis 146
Campanula rotundifolia 31, 33, 145
Campanula rotundifolia 'Alba' 146
Canadian burnett 167
Candytuft 126
Canterbury bells 16, 27, 69, 121
Caraway 93
Cardoon 148
Carex buchananii 14, 59
Carex 'Frosty Curls' 59
Carnation 148
Catananche caerulea 73, 146
Catmint 24, 159
Celosia cristata 121
Centaurea cyanus 121
Centaurea dealbata 146
Centaurea gymnocarpa 146
Centaurea montana 146
Centranthus ruber 16, 33, 35, 82, 146
Centranthus ruber 'Albus' 146
Cerastium tomentosum 16, 31, 146
Chamomile 73, 93
Cheiranthus cheiri 63, 121
Chervil 93
Chinese aster 121
Chinese forget-me-not 54, 58, 124
Chinese mugwort 143
Chinese peony 160
Chinese pink 124
Chinese primrose 83
Chives 93
Christmas rose 156
Chrysanthemum carinatum 72
Chrysanthemum cinerariifolium 146
Chrysanthemum coccineum 33, 59, 63, 72, 146
Chrysanthemum coronarium 123

Chrysanthemum frutescans 14, 31, 33, 72, 89, 147
Chrysanthemum morifolium 31, 33, 147
Chrysanthemum parthenium 31, 59, 147
Chrysanthemum superbum 31, 59, 72, 148
Clarkia amoena 123
Cleome hasslerana 46, 123
Clover 100
Cockspur flower 163
Columbine 54, 77, 142
Common mignonette 76
Compost 105
Coneflower 166
Consolida ambigua 19, 82, 124
Convallaria majalis 31
Convolvulus mauritanicus 82
Coral bells 157
Coriander 93
Corncockle 58, 119
Cornflower 54, 58, 72, 121
Corsican hellebore 156
Cosmos bipinnatus 46, 54, 59, 88, 124
Cosmos 'Red Dazzler' 35
Cottage pink 150
Cotton lavender 167
Crane's bill 154
Cupid's dart 73, 146
Cynara cardunculus 148
Cynoglossum amabile 46, 48, 124

Dahlia hybrids 31, 33, 34, 148
Dahlia imperalis 148
Dahlia, tree 148
Daisy 24
Dalmation bellflower 145
Dandelion 100
Daylily 27, 34, 98, 156
Delphinium 29, 34, 69, 72
Delphinium elatum 'Pacific Giant' 19, 31, 33, 148
Delphinium grandiflorum 19
Dianthus x allwoodii 148
Dianthus barbatus 63, 124
Dianthus caryophyllus 31, 33, 63, 150
Dianthus chinensis 63, 124
Dianthus deltoides 63, 150
Dinathus plumarius 150
Dicentra formosa 150

Dicentra spectabilis 82, 150
Dictamnus albus 31, 150
Dierama pulcherrimum 150
Digitalis ferruginea 150
Digitalis grandiflora 150
Digitalis x heywoodii 150
Digitalis lanata 150
Digitalis lutea 150
Digitalis x mertonensis 150
Digitalis purpurea 31, 33, 54, 69, 82, 151
Digitalis viridflora 151
Dill 93
Doronicum plantagineum 31, 72, 82, 151

Echinacea purpurea 151
Echinops bannaticus 152
Echinops ritro 33, 152
Echium fastuosum 33, 69, 152
English daisy 98, 144
English harebell 145
English primrose 83
Eremurus robustus 19
Erigeron karvinskianus 31, 33, 54, 72, 76, 89, 152
Eryngium maritimum 32, 152
Eschscholzia californica 34, 54, 48, 124
Euphorbia 34
Euphorbia amygdaloides 152
Euphorbia characias 153
Euphorbia epithymoides 153
Euphorbia robbiae 153
Eustoma grandiflora 47
Evening primrose 27, 34, 54, 79, 160
Evening-scented stock 75

Fagus species 51
Fairy fishing rod 150
Fairy grass 155
Feathery amaranth 121
Feeding 108
Felicia amelloides 23, 27, 33, 72, 89, 153
Fennel 93
Festuca ovina 'Glauca' 14, 59
Feverfew 59, 147
Filipendula purpurea 153
Flanders poppies 34, 35, 54, 58, 132
Flannel flower 32

Floss flower 119
Forget-me-not 44, 54, 58, 84, 130
Four o'clock plant 75
Foxglove 15, 28, 34, 54, 58, 69, 72, 150, 151
Foxtail lily 19

Garden pink 150
Gayfeather 158
Gazania x hybrida 31, 33, 154
Gentiana acaulis 33, 154
Gentiana lutea 154
Geranium endressii 154
Geranium himalayense 154
Geranium ibericum 16, 27, 154
Geranium, nutmeg-scented 62
Geranium pratense 14, 28, 33, 154
Geranium robertianum 125
Geranium sanguineum 155
Geranium, scented 61, 69
Geranium, zonal 163
Geum quellyon 33, 155
Giant bellflower 16, 27
Gilia capitata 125
Ginger lily 155
Globe amaranth 126
Globe thistle 152
Goat's beard, 18, 144
Godetia 123
Golden rod 169
Gomphrena globosa 126
Granny's bonnet 58, 142
Guinea flower 157
Gypsophila elegans 46, 126
Gypsophila paniculata 31, 77, 155
Gypsophila repens 31, 155

Heartsease 54, 58
Hedychium flavum 31, 63, 155
Helenium autumnale 31, 155
Helianthemum nummularium 31, 155
Helianthum angustifolium 156
Helianthus annuus 126
Helichrysum bracteatum 126, 156
Helipterum humboldtianum 126
Helipterum manglesii 126

Helipterum roseum 126
Helleborus foetidus 156
Helleborus lividus 156
Helleborus niger 31, 82, 156
Helleborus x orientalis 92, 156
Helleborus species 54, 82
Hemerocallis hybrids 31, 33, 63, 98, 156
Herb Robert 125
Heterocentron elegans 156
Heuchera sanguinea 33, 157
Hibbertia serpyllifolia 31, 157
Himalayan blue poppy 159
Hollyhock 69, 140
Honesty 27, 47, 54, 69, 84, 129
Hosta caerulea 157
Hosta fortunei 157
Hosta lancifolia 157
Hosta plantaginea 31, 157
Hosta sieboldiana 157
Hosta species 63, 82
Houstonia caerulea 33, 157
Houstonia purpurea 158
Hunnemannia fumariifolia 126
Hypericum calycinum 27, 82
Hyssop 93

Iberian crane's bill 14, 27, 28, 154
Iberis amara 128
Iberis umbellata 128
Iceland poppy 54, 132
Impatiens 89
Impatiens balsamina 82, 126
Impatiens wallerana 48, 54, 82, 128
Incarvillea delavayi 157
Indian pink 124
Iris 24
Italian bellflower 80, 141, 145

Jacob's ladder 163
Japanese candelabra primrose 83
Japanese windflower 77, 142

Kniphofia hybrids 19, 31, 33, 69, 157

Laceplant 153
Lady's mantle 140
Lamb's ears 32, 168

Lamium 29
Lamium galeobdolon 24, 80, 82
Larkspur 19, 48, 124
Lathyrus odoratus 63, 128
Lavatera trimestris 129, 157
Lavender 24, 28, 93
Lavender shower 168
Lawn daisy 144
Lemon balm 95
Lenten rose 156
Leopard's bane 72, 151
Liatris spicata 158
Lily 28, 34
Lily turf 84
Limonium latifolium 33, 158
Limonium perezii 158
Limonium sinuatum 129
Linaria maroccana 129
Linaria reticulata 129
Liriope muscari 84
Liriope spicata 82, 84
Lisianthus 47
Lobelia erinus 27, 129
Lobularia maritima 63, 82, 129
London pride 84, 167
Loosestrife 18, 159
Lovehearts 24, 47
Love-in-a-mist 44, 46, 54, 58, 59, 69, 132
Love-lies-bleeding 119
Lunaria annua 27, 47, 48, 54, 69, 82, 84, 129
Lupin 28, 34, 130, 159
Lupinus densiflorus 130
Lupinus hartwegii 31, 33, 129
Lupinus polyphyllus 'Russell Lupins' 18, 82, 158
Lychnis chalcedonica 159
Lychnis coronaria 31, 32, 33, 35, 54, 159
Lythrum salicaria 18, 159

Malcolmia maritima 63, 82, 130
Mallow, annual 129
Malva alcea 159
Malva moschata 159
Marguerite daisy 14, 27, 28, 69, 72, 77, 89, 147
Marigold 88
Marigold, African 134
Marigold, English 88
Marigold, pot 34, 100, 120
Marjoram 93

Marshmallow 141
Maskflower 141
Masterwort 144
Mathiola bicornis 75
Mathiola incana 48, 63, 130
Mathiola longipetala 130
Meconopsis betonicifolia 33, 159
Meconopsis cambrica 160
Meadow crane's bill 14, 154
Medicinal lungwort 165
Melissa officinalis 95
Mexican giant hyssop 140
Michaelmas daisy 77, 143
Mignonette 133
Mirabilis jalapa 75
Molucella laevis 47, 130
Monarda didyma 94
Mondo grass 83, 160
Money plant 129
Monkshood 140
Moonflower 79
Mountain ash 51
Mugwort 94
Mulching 110
Mullein 18, 19, 32, 34, 54, 168
Muskmallow 159
Myosotis sylvatica 48, 82, 130

Nasturtiums 34, 88, 98, 134
Nemesia strumosa 131
Nepeta cataria 159
Nepeta x faassenii 24, 159
Nemophila menziesii 82, 131
Nicotiana alata 47, 63, 75, 82, 131
Nicotiana sylvestris 48, 75, 132
Nierembergia hippomanica 28
Nigella damascena 28, 46, 48, 54, 69, 82, 132
Night-scented tobacco 75
Norwegian snow 145

Oak 51
Obedient plant 162
Oenothera acaulis 76, 160
Oenothera biennis 31, 76, 159
Oenothera odorata 160
Oenothera pallida 160
Oenothera speciosa 76, 160
Ophiopogon jaburan 84
Ophiopogon japonicus 82, 83, 160

Opium poppy 132
Oriental poppy 34, 160
Oyster plant 69, 139
Oxalis acetosella 160
Oxalis magellanica 160
Oxalis versicolor 160

Paeonia lactiflora 31, 33, 160
Paeonia lutea 31
Paeonia suffruticosa 160
Painted tongue 133
Pansy 34, 97, 134
Papaver nudicaule 54, 132
Papaver orientale 31, 33, 160
Papaver rhoeas 35, 54, 132
Papaver somniferum 132
Papaver species 48
Parsley 93
Pasque flower 165
Peach-leaved campanula 145
Pelargonium crispum 62
Pelargonium x domesticum 31, 33, 160
Pelargonium fragrans 62, 161
Pelargonium graveolens 161
Pelargonium x hortorum 31, 33, 161
Pelargonium x nervosum 62
Pelargonium odoratissimum 62, 161
Pelargonium peltatum 161
Pelargonium querciifolium 161
Pelargonium species 63
Pelargonium tomentosum 62
Pennisetum rueppli 59
Penstemon barbatus 161
Penstemon digitalis 162
Penstemon hartwegii 162
Penstemon hirsutus 162
Penstemon hybrids 31, 33, 161
Perennial chrysanthemum 147
Persian knapweed 146
Peruvian lily 141
Petunia x hyrbida 133
Phacelia campanularia 46, 133
Phlox, annual 133
Phlox drummondii 133
Phlox paniculata 31, 33, 82, 162
Phlox, perennial 77, 162

Phlox subulata 31, 162
Physostegia virginiana 82, 162
Pincushion flower 48, 133
Pink cornflower 146
Pink crane's bill 154
Pinks 150
Plantain lily 157
Platycodon grandiflorum 33, 163
Plectranthus ecklonii 163
Plectranthus oertendahlii 80. 82, 163
Polemonium caeruleum 163
Polyanthus species 31, 33, 83, 98, 163
Polygonatum x hybridum 163
Polygonatum multiflorum 31, 82, 163
Polygonatum odoratum 163
Polygonum affine 163
Polygonum bistorta 31, 163
Prickly poppy 143
Pride of China 157
Primrose, japonica 83
Primula auricula 165
Primula denticulata 165
Primula floribunda 83
Primula florindae 165
Primula japonica 165
Primula x kewensis 83
Primula malacoides 48, 54, 82, 133
Primula obconica 165
Primula x polyantha 82, 83, 98, 163
Primula sinensis 83, 165
Primula verticillata 83
Primula vulgaris 83, 165
Pulmonaria officinalis 165
Pulsatilla vulgaris 165
Purple coneflower 151
Pyrethrum 59, 72, 146
Pyrethrum, red 146

Queen Anne's lace 44, 46, 54, 58, 120
Quercus species 51

Red campion 46, 54, 167
Red hot pokers 19, 69, 157
Regal pelargonium 160
Rehmannia elata 165
Reseda odorata 63, 79, 133
Rockcress 143, 144
Romneya coulteri 31, 165

Rose 28, 72, 100
Rose campion 32, 35, 159
Rosemary 93
Rudbeckia californica 31, 167
Rudbeckia fulgida 166
Rue 93

Sage 93, 94
Sage, clary 95
Sage, red 95
Salpiglossis sinuata 133
Salvia argentea 18, 19, 167
Salvia azurea 166
Salvia coccinea 167
Salvia elegans 167
Salvia farinacea 33, 46, 167
Salvia leucantha 167
Salvia officinalis 94, 167
Salvia oficinalis 'Purpurea' 95
Salvia patens 167
Salvia sclarea 95, 167
Salvia uliginosa 167
Sandwort 143
Sanquisorba canadensis 167
Santolina chamaecyparissus 27, 28, 31, 167
Saponaria officinalis 82, 167
Savory 93
Saxifraga umbrosa 33, 82, 84, 167
Scabiosa atropurpurea 48, 133
Scarlet avens 155
Sea holly 152
Sea pink 143
Senecio 'Silver Dust' 28
Shasta daisy 59, 72, 77, 148
Shell flower 130
Shirley poppies 58, 59
Shungiku 123
Silene coeli-rosa 24, 47, 48
Silene dioica 46, 48, 54, 167
Silver birch 51
Snap dragon 34, 120
Sneeze weed 156

Snow in summer 16, 146
Soap wort 167
Soil 103
Solidago canadense 31, 169
Solomon's seal 163
Sorbus aucuparia 51
Southernwood 94
Spanish shawl 156
Speedwell 170
Spiderflower 46, 123
Stachys byzantina 32, 168
Stachys grandiflora 168
Stachys officinalis 168
Statice 129
Stinking hellebore 156
Stock 48, 130
Stoke's aster 72, 77, 89, 168
Stokesia laevis 31, 72, 89, 168
Strawflower 126, 156
Summer forget-me-not 145
Sunflower 34, 73, 126
Sunrose 155
Swan River daisy 14, 72, 89, 145
Sweetpea 128
Sweet William 124

Tagetes species 88
Tagetes erecta 134
Tansy 93
Taraxacum officinale 100
Tassel flower 119
Taxus baccata 51
Thalictrum aquilegifolium 168
Thalictrum dipterocarpum 33, 168
Thrift 143
Thyme 62, 63, 93, 168
Thymus citriodorus 62, 168
Thymus pseudolanuginosus 62
Thymus serpyllum 31, 62, 168
Thymus species 33
Thymus vulgaris 168

Toadflax 59, 129
Tobacco plant 131
Torenia fournieri 48, 82, 134
Tree mallow 157
Tree peony 160
Trifolium species 100
Tropaeolum majus 48, 82, 134
Tulip poppy 126

Valerian, red 16, 35, 146
Verbascum bombyciferum 18, 32, 168
Verbascum chaixii 19, 168
Verbascum chaixii 'Album' 19, 168
Verbena 77
Verbena x hybrida 31, 33, 82, 170
Verbena officinalis 170
Verbena rigida 170
Veronica spicata 33, 170
Viola cornuta 97, 134
Viola hederacea 80, 82, 170
Viola odorata 31, 33, 63, 80, 82, 97, 170
Viola tricolor 48, 134
Viola x wittrockiana 63, 82, 97, 134

Viper's bugloss 69
Virginia stock 130
Viscaria 54, 84

Wallflower 27, 34, 121
Watering 110
Wishbone 48, 134
Woodspurge 152
Wormwood 32, 77, 143

Yarrow 93, 139
Yew 51
Youth and old age 134

Zinnia elegans 46, 134
Zinnia haageana 135

OTHER BOOKS BY CHERYL MADDOCKS
from Doubleday

LET THE GARDEN GO
A ROMANTIC APPROACH TO GARDENING

Let the Garden Go shows how to create a garden gently and guide it. When planted with a combination of bulbs, perennials, annuals and self-seeding plants, your garden will be full of year-round interest and will tend to look after itself.

Let the Garden Go is a rediscovery of the old-fashioned garden. The look is informal, abundant and spontaneous—making the most of natural colour and fragrance.

Cheryl Maddocks, a horticulturist and landscape specialist, combines an extensive knowledge of classical and current garden styles with a practical approach to the creation of gardens which are both functional and romantic.

"The advice is inspired"—Stephanie Dowrick, *Vogue Australia*

"... a book that any garden enthusiast will enjoy."—Robin Richards, *Sunday Times*

"... a book for those who love an informal and very spontaneous garden reminiscent of the beautiful, blowsy cottage gardens of England."—*Australian Home and Garden*

GARDEN INSPIRATIONS
IDEAS FOR EVERY SEASON

A selection of Cheryl Maddocks's writings, *Garden Inspirations* covers 40 topics—from designing a kitchen garden to choosing native plants capable of attracting birds and butterflies. Whether the subject is colour themes, scented gardens, topiary, ornamental grasses or companion planting, *Garden Inspirations* reflects the author's extensive knowledge of both classical and contemporary garden styles. And the book is written with the combination of practicality and imagination which is a feature of all Cheryl's writing. *Garden Inspirations* contains exciting ideas for spring, summer, autumn and winter; it is truly a book for all seasons.

THE SALAD GARDEN

The Salad Garden looks at growing and preparing a delicious variety of salad vegetables, herbs and fruits and investigates new food sources from edible weeds and flowers. In a simple and informative way, the essentials of propagation, planting and maintenance for each vegetable are explained.

The Salad Garden presents 160 easy-to-prepare salad recipes for you to enjoy the fruits of your own labour. These delightful recipes are the culmination of the natural process from garden to table.

Cheryl Maddocks is among Australia's most prolific gardening writers. Apart from gardening, Cheryl's passion is cooking. Cheryl realised the exciting possibilities of creative salad making when she was a chef at a popular vegetarian restaurant in the Blue Mountains.

GARDEN STYLE
A PRACTICAL AUSTRALIAN GUIDE TO CREATING YOUR IDEAL GARDEN

Garden style in Australia has come of age. Australian garden style is now as distinctive as Australian architectural style.

This exciting book encompasses classical, cottage garden and modern styles. Whether you are designing and building a new garden or creating a small, enchanting area in an existing one, *Garden Style* will provide fresh and stimulating ideas.

This comprehensive book consists of three sections. The first, "Garden Styles", contains a broad range of design concepts features in 34 distinctive gardens. The second section, "Creating Your Ideal Garden", provides specific instructions which will enable you to plan and design a garden reflecting your needs and desires. Section three, "Practicalities", features practical information on preparation, propagation and maintenance.